Jewish Presences

Oliver introduced to the respectable Old Gentleman.

Illustration to the original edition of *Oliver Twist*.

Jewish Presences in English Literature

EDITED BY

DEREK COHEN AND

DEBORAH HELLER

McGill-Queen's University Press
Montreal & Kingston • London • Buffalo

© McGill-Queen's University Press 1990
ISBN 0-7735-0781-7

Legal deposit fourth quarter 1990
Bibliothèque nationale du Québec

Printed in Canada on acid-free paper

This book has been published with the help of a
grant from the Canadian Federation for the
Humanities, using funds provided by the Social
Sciences and Humanities Research Council of
Canada.

Material used in chapter 4 appeared in an earlier
form in *The Shakespeare Quarterly* 31, no. 1
(Spring 1980): 53–64. Material used in chapter 7
appeared in an earlier, briefer form as "George
Eliot's Jewish Feminist" in *Atlantis* 8, no. 2
(Spring/Printemps 1983): 37–43.

Canadian Cataloguing in Publication Data

Main entry under title:
Jewish presences in English literature
Includes bibliographical references.
ISBN 0-7735-0781-7
    1. English literature – History and
criticism. 2. Jews in literature. I. Cohen,
Derek. II. Heller, Deborah, 1939-
PR151.J5J49 1990   820.9′35203924
C90-090276-0

This book was typeset by Typo Litho composition
inc. in 10/12 Binny on 2506 picas.

To Anita and Barney Cohen

To Bertha Ann Heller
and the memory of Isaiah Heller
and Jules and Daniel

Contents

viii Contents

Jewish Presences

Introduction

Though Jews have been known for centuries as the People of the Book, books have, more often than not, been unkind to Jews. This study explores the principal ways in which Jews have been depicted in major works of English literature. Literary stereotypes can exert a coercive power because their vitality is that of literature and is not dependent upon empirical verification or coincidence with the world outside of books. Since the effect of literary representations is often to promote confusion between art and life, a more informed awareness of the ways in which literary constructs work may make us less vulnerable to the potential tyranny they exercise over our imaginations. As explorations of female stereotypes in literature have helped to remove lingering confusions regarding the nature of women, so it is to be hoped that this study, by clarifying how English literature has presented the Jew, may help liberate our imaginations to look anew at real Jewish identities with that unbiased vision which, according to George Eliot, is the healthy eye of the soul.

These chapters vary in their approaches, but the authors have in common an interest in the sheer presence of the Jew in English literature and in exploring the uses which have been made of this figure through the centuries. All but one of the chapters focus on a single major writer and present a sustained critical study of one or two major works. Jews have played a notable role in English writing from Chaucer to the present day. The earliest characterization of the Jew was largely contingent on popular superstition, political convenience, and folk mythology. The Jew of medieval and Renaissance literature was, for the most part, a composite of negative characteristics designed to call forth predictable responses. The readmission of Jews to the England of Cromwell made little immediate difference to their literary representation. No longer strangers in English society, but still marginalized by virtue of their unfamiliar religion and small numbers, Jews remained on the outskirts of English society and were depicted as essentially separate from the mainstream. Even positive literary representations of Jews in the nineteenth century emphasize their difference, whereas to the extent that their position in society became increasingly "normalized," Jews were often seen as symptomatic of the decadence brought upon English (and European) society by the capitalist ethic. It was not until the twentieth century that a Jew would take on the role of Everyman.

The image of the Jew in English literature, as in the Western imagination, has at its base the figure of the Christ-killer. All representations of the Jew in Christian culture are constructed in the light of this irreducible definition. It can be expanded and varied, deliberately negated, or overlooked. But the Christ-murderer − sometimes presented as the devil or the devil in disguise − inevitably hovers in the background.

Exploring the different ways in which writers in one tradition have amplified, varied, or denied this original archetype, these essays are unified by their authors' awareness of the common tradition out of which representations of Jews in English literature have developed, and are designed to illustrate high points in the continuity of this tradition as well as its modifications. As in the wider cultural imagination the Jew moved from Christ-murderer to ritual murderer of Christians, so this pattern of association makes itself felt in our literature through Chaucer, Shakespeare, Dickens, and on to Trollope. From ritual murderer to bloodthirsty usurer, to murderous fence, to almost cannibalistic devourer of widows and orphans − each permutation reflects the author's often barely conscious memory of its submerged origin.

This memory is no less present in what might be called the counterbalancing examples, those works in our literature where it is denied or overlooked. It was the imputed "Ur"-crime of the Jews that led to historical anti-Semitism. Some authors in more recent, enlightened times have sought to counteract traditional negative Jewish stereotypes, often with the express purpose of redressing a historical injustice. Thus we have Dickens's good Jew, a carefully structured anti-type of his bad Jew, Eliot's virtuous, prophetic Jews, or Joyce's universalized Jewish Everyman/Outsider. Whatever the variations, every major Jewish character in English literature has been created in the light of his or her literary predecessors.

All the contributors to this collection are keenly aware of the unifying thread in literary representations of Jews in our tradition, but each approaches the material in his or her own fashion. Although no discussion of Jewish presences in English literature can ignore the social context in which such representations developed, in each chapter the emphasis is primarily textual. These are literary critical essays, not essays in social history. Taken collectively they inevitably highlight major trends in the development of a stereotype, but this is not an evolutionary study of the Jew in English literature. Our approach has been selective rather than exhaustive. We have chosen the subjects of our individual studies from the greatest writers in English literature. We are, above all, interested in exploring how Jewish constructs fit into a writer's pre-existing concerns and patterns of representation, and are much less interested in speculations on how and if individual works may have contributed to the view of Jews in society or on what, if anything, literary representations may reveal about a writer's "true" attitudes towards Jews. It is our hope that this book will be read for what it may contribute to the reader's appreciation of the internal dynamics of individual works.

The earliest depiction of a Jewish community in a major work in English is found in Chaucer's *The Prioress's Tale*. Despite the silence of several early twentieth-century critics on the subject, this Tale is clearly and strongly anti-Semitic. How are readers in the late twentieth century to interpret this anti-Semitism? A "pure" reading of the Tale, in which one sees it only as a sentimental example of the common medieval genre of the miracle of the Virgin, is, as Allen Koretsky shows, inadequate. A truer, richer reading will interpret this tale, as it will most others in the Canterbury collection, dramatically; that is, it will consider it in the light of the personality of the teller. The Prioress, one of Chaucer's most challengingly, ambiguous characters, is presented in *The General Prologue* as innocent, childlike, and delicate. How remarkable it is, then, that Chaucer ascribes to her a story full of hatred for the Jews. The primary intention behind this particular match of tale and teller is neither to depict the Prioress as a cruel bigot nor to elicit sympathy for medieval Jewry as a tragic target of prejudice. Instead Chaucer stresses here an important moral point of a more general nature: through the Prioress and her Tale he shows the terrible danger of innocence. Such an interpretation is fully in accordance with Chaucer's abiding interest in the moral problem of innocence and experience.

Shakespeare, on the other hand, seems more interested in different kinds of experience. *The Merchant of Venice* is a tale of intricate sophistication. At its heart is the best-known Jew of English literature, Shylock, the moneylender. At its periphery hover the connected ideologies of Judaism and Christianity. It is Derek Cohen's contention that a major element of this play is a straight-forward religious contest. Christianity, he argues, wins hands down. The triumph of Christianity does not, however, axiomatically make the play anti-Semitic. Cohen's essay discusses a question that is relevant to most essays in the book: What makes a work of art, or any cultural artifact, anti-Semitic?

Fagin, in Dickens's *Oliver Twist*, a character created more than two centuries after Shylock, stands in a direct line of descent from Shakespeare's villain, and echoes the medieval view (expressed by Chaucer's Prioress) of the "cursed Jewes" as kidnappers, mutilators, and murderers of innocent Christian children. Though a fence rather than a usurer, Fagin is in all other ways a compendium of negative Jewish stereotypes which persisted unabated in the literary and popular imagination from the Middle Ages through the early nineteenth century. A quarter of a century after the creation of Fagin, Dickens attempted to neutralize his Jewish villain through the creation of the "good Jew" – Mr Riah in *Our Mutual Friend* – a wholly positive patriarchal figure who, in contrast to Fagin, acts as a friend and protector of menaced innocent children. Deborah Heller's chapter on Dickens explores these contrasting stereotypes, at the same time showing how Jews define their natures in terms of the conflict between innocence and evil which preoccupied Dickens throughout his fiction, and how a study of Dickens's two most important Jewish characters can help us chart the changes in Dickens's view of evil and his attitude toward society.

In Trollope's *The Way We Live Now*, the problem of the Jew as a conventional villain is compounded by the fact that the whole society of the novel is shot through with corruption. The Jewish villain is merely the most capable criminal in a host of would-be thieves and knaves. And yet the stereotype, modernized and urbanized, lingers on. Even in late nineteenth-century England the Jew is a bit of a wizard, a financial virtuoso, and an avid seeker after power. Trollope's genius invests his Jew with powerful psychological realism. But, as usual, it is a realism that is largely contingent upon a series of ancient responses that have validity only in mythology. The charismatic villain is made to seem more wicked by his possession of a violent, restless desire to subdue the world around him. And he very nearly succeeds, failing in the end not because of any residual virtue in England, but rather because of his own miscalculations. Society is rotten, and the disturbing fact that Jews can attain power within it testifies to its corruption. The novel, on a political level, is a vatic monition that the Jewish stranglehold is tightening, as the essay by Derek Cohen shows.

George Eliot's *Daniel Deronda* differs from these earlier works in that it is quite specifically — and knowledgeably — concerned with Judaism and questions of Jewish identity. Still, the most prominent Jews in it are viewed in such a favourable — indeed, idealized — light that they may be said to constitute a new kind of positive Jewish stereotype. Eliot's novel celebrates a very different set of virtues from the humility, long-standing suffering, and financial and human integrity exemplified by Dickens's Mr Riah and the tradition of the "good Jew" to which he belongs. The most favourably rendered Jewish characters in *Daniel Deronda* are marked by their artistic genius, wide intellectual horizons, idealism, and prophetic zeal; more specifically, the novel is seriously concerned with what today we would call the "Zionist" ideal. The novel juxtaposes two separate yet related plots in which, it has been generally accepted, contemporary English society emerges as morally unsavoury but brilliantly artistically rendered, and the Jewish elements are morally laudable but artistically unsatisfying. Without challenging the essential validity of this judgment, Deborah Heller's essay suggests that it ignores Eliot's use of negative as well as positive stereotypes and, more importantly, that it overlooks the problematic role of the hero's non-stereotypical Jewish mother; through Deronda's mother George Eliot suggests an awareness of the position of women in Jewish culture and tradition that is questioning, if not actually critical, and her eloquent presence in the novel may ultimately prevent it from being as idealizing of Jewish life as it is generally taken — and was consciously intended — to be.

All of these Jews have so far been presented as "other," eccentric types who were all superlatively something — whether villain (most frequently), patriarch, prophet, grand financier, or *grande artiste*. In the face of this tradition James Joyce chose to

make his Jew an Everyman, *l'homme moyen sensuel*, as Harry
Girling shows. Leopold Bloom, the Jew in James Joyce's *Ulysses*, never denies his Jewishness, though he only discovers what
it means to him by reacting to the attitudes of his fellow citizens
of Dublin, gentiles all. Lacking the rudiments of religion or
traces of a traditional upbringing, Bloom has to accept the version of Jewish identity that is reflected in the eyes and expressed
in the judgments of other people. Bloom discovers what it is to
be a Jew at the same time as the reader discovers what it is to
be human, for Joyce reveals the inner theatre of thoughts and
desires even more vividly than the outer area of noble aspirations and randy appetites. This Dublin Jew becomes everyone
who has sinned and suffered and survived. In the course of a
single day, 16 June 1904, we witness birth and death, masturbation, fornication and defecation, we watch Bloom eating a
kidney, rescuing a friend, defying a bully, and exposing his lickerish lust. Whatever normal life consists of is all there, every
public posture and private vice, each variety of affection and
love. But not hate, not horror or catastrophe. Leopold Bloom
exemplifies the ordinariness, the banality of goodness and decency that has preserved those of us who are fortunate enough
to be survivors.

Ross Arthur's essay deals not with one text, but with a selection of works from the ninth to the sixteenth century. He argues
that Jews in medieval literature are not used to say anything
about Jews and Judaism but to deliver a Christian message to
Christian audiences. Arthur shows how some of the texts make
particular points relating to Christian doctrine, and how all the
texts follow a basic pattern. This pattern was not unique to
narratives with Jewish characters but was used in a variety of
contexts throughout the period. Only with the rise of Renaissance individualism were Jews first excluded from this pattern
and portrayed in the familiar stereotypes. In the conclusion of
the piece, Arthur suggests that the problem of Jews in literature
is part of the problem of the ways in which formulaic patterns
and stereotypes in literature can function as mechanisms of
social control.

Jewish Presences covers about seven hundred years of English
literary history. Its range distinguishes this work from the most
important previous study of Jews in English literature, Edgar
Rosenberg's *From Shylock to Svengali* (1960), which focuses on
the late eighteenth and nineteenth centuries. Moreover, while
Rosenberg's critical interpretations of individual works are in-

formed and provocative, they do not claim to be definitive. Where we treat some of the same texts, our analyses offer new perspectives on the material. (Every generation has to recover the past anew and in its own terms.) Montagu Frank Modder's *The Jew in the Literature of England* (1939), a pioneering study, presented an overview of the subject without sustained critical analysis of individual works. Two more recent books, Harold Fisch's *The Dual Image* (1971) and Esther L. Panitz's *The Alien in Their Midst* (1981), while sophisticated in critical awareness and extensive in historical scope, are likewise intended principally to present broad historical surveys of the subject rather than in-depth literary explorations of single texts.

While some of the stereotypical patterns of Jewish identity discussed in this study remain identifiable in contemporary writing, various developments in our century have contributed to altering the ways in which Jews appear in literature. The progressive tendency toward assimilation and "normalization" of the Jew in British and American society, though not in itself sufficient to eradicate stereotypes that have persisted for centuries, has inevitably had some effect in blunting their edge. This "normalization," however, was gravely qualified by the Jewish experience of World War II, with its concomitant rekindling of ethnic self-awareness among Jews, and its legacy of heightened sensitivity to the dangers of stereotypical representation within the non-Jewish world. At the same time, the mass murder of the European Jews has extended the image of the Jew as victim, as universal scapegoat. This image, added to the widespread status of the Jew as displaced person, uprooted refugee or e/immigrant, has, in turn, echoed the sadly generalized experience of many diverse groups throughout the twentieth century, especially in the wake of the dislocations attendant upon two world wars. All these factors have contributed to the creation of a new kind of Jewish stereotype. The Jew's rootlessness, once a distinctive component of his identity, has now become an emblem of contemporary experience.

Derek Cohen
Deborah Heller

CHAPTER ONE

Dangerous Innocence: Chaucer's Prioress and Her Tale

ALLEN C. KORETSKY

The question surely is not whether there is anti-Semitism in *The Prioress's Tale*, but rather how we, in the late twentieth century, are to interpret the strong anti-Semitism that is there.[1] Despite the silence of some earlier, perhaps more genteel, critics who may have intended to match the Prioress's own putative gentility by politely skipping over the anti-Semitism,[2] we cannot deny that the Prioress expresses an unmistakable hatred of Jews. Instead of disregarding this element in the Tale, we can perhaps make a more constructive contribution to Chaucer criticism by attempting to understand why Chaucer included it in the story assigned to Madame Eglantyne. I shall argue that through the moral ambiguity embodied in the Prioress and her Tale the poet is examining the timeless moral problem of innocence and responsibility.

The plot of the Tale centres around the murder of an innocent young Christian boy by wicked Jews. For their terrible crime the Jews suffer severe punishment, and the narrator seems to take great satisfaction in describing that punishment. The epithet "cursed" is applied to Jews several times (ll. 570, 631, 685).[3] Satan is said to make his nest in the Jews' heart (ll. 558–9). Finally, after her story of the murder in the great city "in Asye," the Prioress adds a gratuitous reference to Hugh of Lincoln, who was "slayn also/With cursed Jews" (ll. 684–5). Although *The Prioress's Tale* is not, strictly speaking, the story of a ritual murder, one can easily see in it precisely the kind of passions that were aroused by the widespread medieval ritual murder libel. It was rumoured that Jews killed innocent Christian children to use the blood for their own religious ceremonies.

Today the anti-Semitism of *The Prioress's Tale* is sometimes inconvenient, sometimes downright offensive. It disturbs the cherished modern view of Chaucer as a genial, humane author. Consequently the anti-Semitism of this Tale has either been completely ignored, as noted above, or it has been excused, explained, or palliated in a number of ways. General and literary historians have reminded us that anti-Semitism was rife in the Middle Ages.[4] For some readers it follows from this observation that the Prioress was no worse for hating Jews than most of her contemporaries, including ecclesiastics. One variation of this argument observes that Chaucer himself was a man of his time and that he naturally shared the prejudices of his day, including anti-Semitism.[5] It has been shown, moreover, that anti-Semitism is a common feature of the genre *The Prioress's Tale* exemplifies, the miracle of the Virgin,[6] and that the narrator is exculpable on those grounds. Some critics have pointed out that aspersions against the Jews are to be found in other Chaucerian tales and that it is, therefore, unfair to condemn the Prioress if one does not also condemn the other tellers, most notably the Parson, a character generally regarded as a Christian ideal. Moreover, several readers have noted that the Jews were expelled from England in 1290, that the Prioress, for this reason, had almost certainly never met a Jew, and, therefore, that whatever anti-Semitism there might be in her Tale is not a personal response to real Jews, but rather a literary convention.[7] Finally, it has been argued that to stress the anti-Semitism in the Tale is to miss the point, to distort the author's proportions. Seeing the Tale in its proper generic and historical context, so this argument runs, the modern reader should appreciate the piety induced by the miraculous intervention it describes rather than worry about the wicked Jews, who are, after all, a mere plot convenience: "The wicked, alas, have to be brought into the picture, not so much as foils but as persecutors, i.e. as indispensable agents in the saints' progress toward heaven."[8]

While there is some plausibility in these arguments, I think they fail to provide a complete or even adequate defence of the Prioress, and they lead to a thin reading of the Tale. I believe it is wiser to recognize and confront the essential anti-Semitism in *The Prioress's Tale*, and to try to understand what Chaucer achieved by assigning such a tale, with its essential anti-Semitism, to the Prioress. Read in this way, the Tale has a moral complexity that is characteristic of Chaucer. In my view a reading which sees the anti-Semitism in a pious legend told by an innocent woman is not only valid but is also far more interesting than a reading which ignores, denies, or downplays the anti-Semitism. (In his chapter on Shakespeare and Shylock, Derek

Cohen takes up similar questions with regard to *The Merchant of Venice*. That play and this Tale occupy solid and honoured positions in the still dominant English canon, and both are still used to attack and defend their authors.)

Recognizing the anti-Semitism in the Prioress's story does not necessarily lead to the extreme conclusion postulated by one of her more recent defenders, Albert B. Friedman. He claims that her critics depict her as a "childish, uncharitable, malicious, cruel-minded bigot unworthy of her profession and her office."[9] Friedman here seems to be creating a straw man. One can find the Prioress wanting in moral sophistication without concluding that she is a "malicious, cruel-minded bigot." The vices that Friedman says the Prioress's critics attribute to her are not indivisible. It is possible, for instance, to be childish without being malicious.

The modern reader's response to the Prioress raises a fundamental question about the very nature of Chaucer's characterization. While it is true that Chaucer's verisimilitude may induce the modern reader to see the Prioress as a "real person," as Kittredge, Sister Madeleva, and Manly do,[10] another, subtler way of reading this and other Chaucerian characters stresses their symbolic function: the fictional character is not so much a "real person" as a means of showing real attitudes and values. These two different ways of reading characters — one that emphasizes mimesis and the other that sees what D.W. Robertson, Jr, calls "'characterization' by means of iconographic detail"[11] — are not mutually exclusive. In my view it is silly to deny that Chaucer is creating the illusion that his pilgrims are realistic roadside characters with recognizable personalities, virtues, and faults. On the other hand, the Prioress appears to be even more interesting and effective when seen, not as a rounded "real person," but as a symbol of certain circumstances and attitudes through which the poet poses moral problems.

What kind of morality can be legitimately extracted today from a conventional literary genre of the Middle Ages? Whatever else it may be, *The Prioress's Tale* is an example of a class of a tale known as the miracle of the Virgin. To medieval and modern audiences the primary import of such a tale would doubtless be very different. The essence of such stories is, by definition, the miraculous intervention of the Blessed Virgin Mary in aid of a beleaguered martyr. That is what the Prioress wished to emphasize when she agreed to answer Harry Bailey's request for a tale. Many modern readers, however, have clearly been disturbed by the virulent anti-Semitism in the Tale. Whether Chaucer was also disturbed by this element and whether he was using it to characterize the teller are fair questions. It is hardly revolutionary or even novel to argue that Chaucer often created a discrepancy between a pilgrim narrator's attitude to the material of a story and his own attitude to that same material in order to make a moral point.

What does seem to be beyond dispute is the fundamental historical fact of anti-Semitism in the genre of the miracle of the Virgin. Robert Worth Frank, Jr, has shown, in reference to several collections, both published and in manuscript, in Latin and the vernaculars, that anti-Semitism abounds in various examples of the genre. Frank remarks that "anyone who reads at all extensively in the genre to which Chaucer's tale [i.e. *The Prioress's Tale*] belongs, the miracles of the Virgin, soon becomes aware of the persistent presence of anti-Semitism."[12] This assertion is borne out by examples from Beverly Boyd's collection *The Middle English Miracles of the Virgin*. In three short religious tales published by Boyd and taken from the Vernon manuscript, which is contemporary with Chaucer, being dated 1370 to 1400,[13] Jews are portrayed as cruel, malicious enemies of Christians. One of these fictional Jews is intent upon killing an innocent Christian lad ("The Child Slain by Jews"); another would murder a young convert to Christianity ("The Jewish Boy"). In "The Merchant's Surety" the Jew is exposed as a liar who betrays his Christian friend by falsely denying that he received his payment of a loan. The only good Jews are those who convert to Christianity, as in "The Jewish Boy." Yet, for all their bigoted stereotyping of Jews, tales from the Vernon manuscript are essentially pious stories which lavishly praise

> The blisful qwen, that maiden milde,
> That sitteth in chirche in hih chayer
> With that comely kyng, hire childe.
> ("The Jewish Boy," ll. 156–8)

Apparently the tellers of these miracles, like Chaucer's Prioress, saw no incongruity between reverence for the Blessed Virgin Mary and harsh anti-Semitic portrayals of Jews. This is shown in the work of both Boyd and Frank, which establishes that there is an odd blend of devotion and prejudice in many examples of the genre.

The conjunction of Christian piety and anti-Semitism in the late Middle Ages should come as no surprise to those who see anti-Judaic sentiment as an inherent element of early Christian

history. The contemporary Catholic theologian Gregory Baum
noted in his introduction to Rosemary Ruether's *Faith and Fratricide,* "I had to admit in the course of my study that many biblical
passages reflected the conflict between Church and Synagogue
in the first century."[14] Conflict was inevitable once the Church
proclaimed Jesus as the Messiah and Judaism refused to accept
the proposition: "It was, therefore, almost from the beginning
that the Christian affirmation of Jesus as the Christ was accompanied by a refutation of the synagogal reading of the Scriptures.
This accompanying refutation ... is the source and origin of
Christian anti-Semitism ... The Jews, according to this Christian
refutation, were attached to the letter, to externals, to the shell,
while the Christians were open to the spirit, the inward content,
the deeper meaning of God's promises."[15]

Rosemary Ruether traces the anti-Jewish thinking of early
Christians back to the first Church Fathers and the New Testament. In her study of the *adversos Judaeos* tracts, Ruether
refers to Origen, Augustine, Isidore, and others, all of whom
wrote negatively about the Jews. She quotes extensively from
St John Chrysostom's vitriolic sermons in which he accuses the
Jews of a wide variety of faults, sins, and crimes – of arrogance,
gluttony, lawlessness, and, above all, of killing Christ.[16] When
Chaucer's Prioress claims that the serpent Satan makes his
home in Jews' hearts (ll. 558–9), she is echoing the words of
Chrysostom, spoken a thousand years earlier, that "demons in-
habit the very souls of the Jews."[17]

While the *adversos Judaeos* tracts of the Church Fathers explain the doctrinal basis of Christian anti-Semitism, the state
was also responsible for driving a wedge between Christians
and Jews. A law of Constantius, which dates from 339, prohib-
ited intermarriage, "lest the Jews induce Christian women to
share their shameful lives. If they do this, they will subject
themselves to a sentence of death."[18] Almost a millenium later
this fear of contamination of Christians by Jews is evident in a
legal code compiled in Spain: "We forbid any Jew to keep Christian men or women in his house, to be served by them; although
he may have them to cultivate and take care of his lands, or
protect him on the way when he is compelled to go to some
dangerous place. Moreover, we forbid any Christian man or
woman to invite a Jew or Jewess, or to accept any invitation
from them to eat or drink together, or to drink any wine made
by their hands."[19] Such laws further isolated the Jewish people,
who had long been regarded as different because of their reli-

gious beliefs and customs and the strange language in which
they practised their rituals.

Another reason for anti-Semitism was the medieval Jews'
practice of usury. Although Jews engaged in many trades and
occupations during the Middle Ages, their most distinctive economic activity was lending money for interest. Money was
needed by kings and other nobles to wage wars and by ecclesiastics to build churches and cathedrals. Since the Catholic
Church forbade Christians to practice usury, this activity was
left to the Jews. They were thus caught in an unjust predica-
ment: excluded from many forms of economic employment, they
were allowed by Christians, who needed money, to practise
usury, and then they were abused by Christians for doing so.

The antipathy of medieval Christians toward the Jews had
developed for a variety of reasons – doctrinal, legal, social, and
economic. It was aggravated by the religious zeal of the First
Crusade in 1096, an event that marked an unhappy turning-
point in the history of medieval Jewry. Swept up in the fervour
of the Holy War, unruly mobs in Worms, Mainz, and Prague
massacred Jews and pillaged their communities. Thousands fell
in these slaughters. In Cologne, faced with the choice of being
baptized or killed, many Jews took their own lives.

At about this time the malicious idea of ritual murder, according to which the Jews murder innocent Christian children
in order to use their blood for ritual purposes, began to circulate.
One alleged case had been reported in Norwich, England, in
the twelfth century. The most famous English example of this
accusation, however, is the one involving Hugh of Lincoln, a
boy said to have been murdered by the Jews in 1255, for which
allegation eighteen Jews were put to death. As noted earlier,
the Prioress tacks on to her Tale a reference to this alleged
murder.

The Norwich incident notwithstanding, Jews had lived peace-
fully in England through most of the twelfth century. However,
on the day in 1189 that Richard I was crowned, a London mob,
incited by a false rumour that the King had ordered an assault
against the Jews, began attacking. Many were killed. Richard
had three of the ringleaders put to death and issued a procla-
mation forbidding anyone to molest Jews. But, as soon as
Richard left England to go on crusade, in the spring of 1190, a
gang attacked the Jewish community in the city of York. The
Jews there took refuge in a royal castle. Besieged, without food
or weapons, and realizing that they could not hold out long, they

committed mass suicide. The history of the Jews in medieval England virtually ended when, on 18 July 1290, Edward I issued a decree ordering Jews to leave the country within three months.

Matters on the Continent durig this period were no better. The twelfth century saw the beginning of Jewish ghettoes. Residential segregation led naturally to ignorance regarding Jews, and ignorance to suspicion and hostility. Although the most violent attacks on Jews in late medieval Europe were perpetrated by mobs from the lower orders of society, the official Church was not wholly blameless. While it is true that the Third Lateran Council in 1179 called for the toleration of Jews "on grounds of humanity alone" ("*pro sola humanitate*"), the Fourth Lateran Council of 1215 ordered Jews to wear a token identifying them as Jews. The most familiar form of this token was a yellow badge. Cecil Roth has explained how devastating this decree was: "The culminative result of all this was to stigmatize the Jews in perpetuity as a race of pariahs, to single out isolated individuals for continual insult, and the whole community for attack and massacre on any outburst of popular feeling."[20]

One of the most calamitous events ever to strike Europe occurred in the fourteenth century. The Black Death arrived from Asia in the middle of the century, swept the Continent, and then crossed the Channel to England. Faced with the ravages of this terrible and implacable disease, men and women groped for an explanation. While some saw the affliction as a sign of God's displeasure with human indulgence, others sought a more immediate earthly cause. Not surprisingly, the finger of accusation pointed to those stubborn resisters — those strange and impious outcasts from medieval Christendom who had defied the Church and its teachings. Specifically, the Jews were charged with poisoning the drinking water in wells and thus causing the pestilence. Such accusations were, like the charge of ritual murder, utterly absurd and illogical (Jews also died of the Black Death), but they fitted well into the general climate of anti-Semitism and led to further persecutions of Jews.[21] These libels were to have repercussions through the centuries; they contributed to the image of Jews both in the popular imagination and in literary representations, as subsequent chapters will show.

This, then, was the historical background against which Chaucer's Prioress told her Tale. Whether such a background excuses the Prioress for her strong anti-Semitism is a crucial question. We may find at least part of the answer by looking elsewhere in Chaucer.

Some other Chaucerian narrators do, in fact, refer to Jews. Far from justifying the Prioress's anti-Semitism, however, these references underline, by contrast, the especially vitriolic nature of the Prioress's attitude. *The Chaucer Concordance* reports twenty-two occurrences of the word *Jewry* or *Jew* in the poet's corpus. Ten of these are in *The Prioress's Tale*. The other references are scattered through the following works: *The House of Fame* (2), *Sir Thopas* (1), *The Monk's Tale* (2), *The Pardoner's Tale* (2), *The Parson's Tale* (4), and *The Astrolabe* (1).

Most of these other references to Jews are either neutral or mildly favourable. In *The House of Fame* the narrator says that he sees standing on a pillar

> The Ebrayk Josephus, the olde
> That of Jewes gestes tolde;
> And he bar on hys shuldres hye
> The Fame up of the Jewerye.
> (ll. 1433–6)

In *The Tale of Sir Thopas* the narrator reports that the hero's "fyn hawberk, / Was al ywrought of Jewes werk" (ll. 863–4). The Monk, in relating the story of King Antiochus, tells the events from a Jewish point of view and shows the bad end that the enemy of the Jews suffered. He refers to Jews as "Goddes peple" (l. 2588). In the Prologue to *The Treatise on the Astrolabe*, Chaucer tells his son that the conclusions that he is about to pass on to him have previously been rendered in Greek, Arabic, and "to Jewes in Ebrew" (l. 32). The Pardoner boasts that one of his relics is a "sholder-boon/Which that was of an hooly Jewes sheep" (ll. 350–1). A few lines later he refers to "thilke hooly Jew" (l. 364) who taught his people how to increase their livestock.

Despite the widespread anti-Semitism of Chaucer's day, there is no trace of anti-Semitic feeling in these references. There is no hostility to or disapproval of the Jews or their works in these lines. On the contrary, they show recognition of the holy biblical history of the Jewish people, their learning, and their skill in crafts. Chaucer's own poetry thus invalidates the argument that Chaucerian characters must necessarily be anti-Semitic because they live in anti-Semitic times.

One must, however, acknowledge another, much harsher kind of reference to Jews in Chaucer. Both the Pardoner and the Parson refer to the Jews as Christ-killers. But with neither of these men is the anti-Jewish feeling central or essential to their main arguments. In both tales allusions to the Jews are incidental to their intentions. When these ecclesiastics refer to Jews, they are warning their Christian listeners against swearing. Introducing his group of rioters, the Pardoner notes that swearing is one of their many vices. (Swearing was traditionally thought to tear to pieces the body of Christ):

> Hir othes been so grete and so dampnable
> That it is grisly for to heere hem swere.
> Oure blissed Lordes body they totere –
> Hem thoughte that Jewes rente hym noght ynough.
> (ll. 472–5)

This reference to the Jews, a single line, is thus only a passing allusion. Later, while exposing the vice of swearing, the Parson refers antagonistically to the Jews, calling them a "cursede" people who dismembered the body of Christ (l. 590; cf., l. 599). In view of the Parson's reputation as one of Chaucer's noblest characters, we may be inclined to think that the Parson's censure of the Jews has some moral authority. In interpreting this reference, however, it is important to note context and proportion. The Parson makes his brief allusion to the Jews during an earnest condemnation of swearing, which comes under the larger sin of wrath. The references to the Jews in the Parson's sermon, therefore, are proportionately far less significant than the anti-Semitic remarks of the Prioress in her Tale. Not only are there fewer remarks about Jews in the much longer *Parson's Tale*; there is a significant difference in quality as well. In *The Parson's Tale* there is nothing like the Prioress's report of the murder of an innocent child, nor does the Parson display the Prioress's vindictive satisfaction in seeing the Jews punished.

Exculpation of the Prioress's anti-Semitism on the grounds of literary convention is also ultimately unacceptable. To be sure, the genre of the Tale and the anti-Semitism in it are, as we have seen, conventional. But conventional is not the same as essential. Although Robert Worth Frank does establish the widespread occurrence of anti-Semitism in the genre of the miracle of the Virgin, he also shows that anti-Semitism is far from universal in these stories: "Of the twenty-seven manuscript collections listed in Ward ... Latin, French, Anglo-Norman, and English, only three have no anti-Semitic tales. The collections contain five to ninety-three items; of the total, 9 percent of the

tales are anti-Semitic. Evelyn Faye Wilson indexes a total of
146 individual legends, including the ten anti-Semitic miracles
that occur most frequently and an eleventh ... only slightly less
popular. This gives us 7½ percent as a rough figure."[22] In other
words, though anti-Semitism may be a common element in the
miracle of the Virgin, it is hardly a necessary one. The presence
of anti-Semitism in *The Prioress's Tale*, it follows, represents a
choice, if not on the Prioress's part, then on Chaucer's.

Furthermore, unquestioning acceptance of *The Prioress's Tale*
on the grounds of literary convention alone does not accord with
received critical opinion about Chaucer's attitude toward, and
treatment of, literary convention in most of his other major
works of poetry. Chaucer was no slavish follower of literary
convention. On the contrary, his high critical reputation today
is due in large part to his free play with convention, his fresh
adaptation of old motifs and genres. Therefore, the argument
that *The Prioress's Tale* had to be anti-Semitic because anti-
Semitism was conventional in many of the miracles of the Virgin
is simply not tenable.

Nor can one argue that a skeptical reading of the Prioress and
her Tale necessarily makes Chaucer un-Christian or anti-Christian; such a reading no more makes Chaucer censorious of the
Church than the unflattering portraits of the Friar, Pardoner,
and Summoner do. Satiric portraits of clerical figures, far from
showing contempt for the Church, express respect for it and
anger at those who abuse ecclesiastical office.

Like most other satirical authors, Chaucer was a deeply moral
writer, and a philosophical consideration of the Prioress's story
raises an interesting question about her moral responsibility.
Despite the anti-referential tendency of some modern literary
theory, the fact remains that words in a story refer to real things
and circumstances outside of the literary world. When speaking
about Jews, the Prioress, however parochial she may be, is referring to a real historical people who, in her own times, suffered
tragic persecution in various parts of Europe. The Prioress
speaks of Jewish ghettoes and usury, and, at the conclusion of
her tale, she refers to the libel concerning Hugh of Lincoln. All
of these things – ghettoes, usury, the libel of ritual murder –
are facts of history. Either the Prioress is aware of the social
realities that her words point to, or she is not. If the former,
then she is unsympathetically referring to a minority that in her
own lifetime was subjected to restrictions, defamations, and
worse; if the latter, then she does not fully know what she is

talking about. In either case she shows no regret over the prejudicial effect of her words on her listeners. If anything, her words will serve to reinforce and inflame anti-Semitic prejudice.

One possible response to such a critical approach is that it sounds hopelessly modern. The Prioress, after all, is a simple medieval woman. She thinks she is telling a pious miracle, and of course she is. But she is also casting aspersions on the Jews, repeating old anti-Semitic libels, and thus perpetuating a vicious prejudice. From time to time this sentiment erupted in Europe, causing unjust hardship, injury, and death to countless Jews.

We now come to the central moral questions raised by the Prioress and her Tale: is she responsible for the nasty anti-Semitism in her story, or should her innocence protect her from any censure by modern readers? Furthermore, to what extent does innocence diminish one's authority to pronounce on moral matters? If innocence absolves one from moral responsibility, does it not also to some extent limit adult emotional capacity and the moral feelings that spring from it?

Chaucer was interested in these questions. A serious if genial moralist, he had explored the problem of innocence and love from his earliest narrative poems. In the minor poems he generally treated his innocent narrators with ironic good humour. The ultimate meaning of the inadequate narrators in these poems is elusive. They are an early example of what Florence Ridley calls Chaucer's "intentional ambiguity." Ridley reminds us that "Chaucer almost never tells us specifically what he means, but he has left us with an open-endedness which invites endless divergent interpretations."[23] Critics are still arguing about the personality and perceptiveness of the dreamer-narrator in *The Book of the Duchess*. Does he or does he not understand the Black Knight? Does he in fact understand the experience of love? In poking fun at the narrator of *The House of Fame*, Chaucer raises weighty philosophical questions in a charming, lighthearted vein: How does one learn about love, this most profound of human experiences? Indeed, how does one learn the truth about anything, Chaucer asks in this playful epistemological poem. The poet laughs at the absurd discrepancy embodied in a narrator who, as the Eagle teasingly reminds him, endeavours

To make bookys, songes, dytees,
In ryme, or elles in cadence,

As thou best canst, in reverence
Of Love, and of hys servantes eke,
....
Although thou haddest never part. (ll. 622–28)

Throughout most of this poem the narrator is passive. He learns about love from his books, of course, and also as a pupil of the Eagle and as a spectator in the domain of Fame. In *The Parlement of Foules* the role of the earnest, bookish narrator is also that of a spectator. Whatever Chaucer may be telling us about love in these poems, the narrators – like the narrator of *Troilus*, but unlike the hero of that romance – are not depicted as deeply involved in the experience. In these works the poet rather than the narrator is the chief moral authority.

To be sure, the kind of love the Prioress is illustrating in her Tale is very different from the erotic love illustrated in the minor narrative poems, though in medieval times the line between religious and secular love was not so sharp as it is today. The ambiguity of the word *"amor"* in the motto on the Prioress's brooch is one of the most celebrated *cruces* of modern Chaucer criticism.[24] Given the portrait of the Prioress in the General Prologue, we may wonder what kind of love she has felt, beyond her sentimental pity for mice and dogs; and, indeed, more importantly, we wonder whether she has the capacity for profound adult love. It is true that the eloquent invocation to Mary preceding her Tale does express one kind of love, the humble devotion of a pious Christian to the unseen Mother of Christ. This of course is quite different from the love of one human being for another. Within the story the "litel clergeoun" is also devoted to Christ's mother: "This welle of mercy, Cristes mooder sweete, / I loved alwey, as after my konnynge" (ll. 656–7). The most poignant love in the Tale, however, is plainly that of the bereaved mother, "This newe Rachel" (l. 627), for her slain child. If we grant the sincerity of the professions of Christian devotion in the Tale (and there is no need to doubt it), and if we acknowledge the poignancy of the account of maternal love, then we must also note that these passages stand in marked contrast to those that display the virulent hatred of the Jews.

Like most of the other Canterbury stories, *The Prioress's Tale*, in order to be fully appreciated, must be seen in its dramatic context. Taken out of this context, *The Prioress's Tale* would certainly be less problematic (though the inherent contradictions in it between sweetness and hatred, piety and vengeance, would still present considerable difficulty for the modern reader); but then, taken out of dramatic context, this story and all the others in the Canterbury collection would be far less interesting as literature and as expressions of human personality. The point is that Chaucer chose to give all the stories in *The Canterbury Tales* a dramatic context, and he has taken some pains with the characterizations of many of the tellers, including the Prioress. The problem with reading *The Prioress's Tale* as simply an example of a pure devotional narrative is that such a reading leaves out far too much that is significant. It ignores the rich dramatic function of the Tale, a function that readers cheerfully and readily assume when discussing, say, *The Knight's Tale*, *The Wife of Bath's Tale*, or *The Merchant's Tale*. Any "pure" reading of the Prioress's story would forfeit the intriguing ambiguity in the personality of the teller, an ambiguity that is doubtless the most challenging feature of her portrait. Without for a moment denying the piety and touches of beauty in the Tale, the modern reader cannot help but also see several disturbing elements that jar incongruously with the Tale's dominant tone of sweet religiosity. In a Tale that stresses pious devotion to the Mother of Christ, the narrator apparently rejoices in the violent retribution inflicted on the Jews, and the modern critic must have the right to consider the moral meaning of the Prioress's apparent relish in recounting the Jews' "shameful deeth" (l. 628). The incongruity is aesthetic as well as moral. For all her presumed delicacy the Prioress makes a strange reference to a "wardrobe ... where as thise Jewes purgen hire entraille" (ll. 572–3). Again the modern critic is entitled at least to wonder about the meaning of such an unpleasant scatological reference.[25]

Alfred David has given us one of the more persuasive interpretations of the Prioress. Her immaturity, he suggests, is the key to understanding her personality and her story: her inexperience of the world, sentimentality, and concern with outward appearance make Madame Eglantyne a less than fully grown human being. David believes it is entirely fitting that the kind of story this child-woman chooses to tell is, in essence, a "fairy story that has been turned into hagiography."[26]

While accepting the plausibility of David's reading, I should like to add to it by suggesting that there may be special significance to the fact that Chaucer chooses the Prioress, of all people, to tell this harshly anti-Semitic tale. Certainly it is noteworthy that Chaucer assigns to the sheltered, fastidious

Prioress the most sustained, virulent outpouring of anti-Semitic prejudice in his whole corpus. Although the genre of the miracle does fit the Prioress, the rougher elements of the Tale – the scatological reference and the bloody account of retribution – might seem more appropriate to such a character as the loutish Miller, the crabbed Reeve, or the nasty Merchant. By assigning this Tale instead to a representative of the Church, and a very innocent one at that, Chaucer may be commenting on both the Church and innocence. He may well be suggesting that the Church has a special responsibility not only to promulgate the legends of the faith but also to be cognizant of the perils attendant on zeal. A master of irony, Chaucer has created the appalling irony of a seemingly gentle nun preaching hatred while expressing her devotion to the mother of Christ. Chaucer had not been loath to show through other clerics on the Canterbury pilgrimage the abuse of ecclesiastical office, and *The Prioress's Tale*, for all its piety, illustrates the most un-Christian passion of hatred in the very name of that piety.

Finally there is the terrible danger of innocence. In his discussion of the Prioress's childlike imagination Alfred David notes that for her "The fact is that the 'cursed Jews' represent a psychological rather than a historical reality. They are symbols of pure evil, and they belong to the large class of fairy-tale villains, which includes all kinds of monsters and ogres as well as witches, devils, and wicked stepmothers and stepsisters."[27] To some this might well be an adequate explanation and exculpation of the Prioress's anti-Semitism: it is not to be taken seriously because Jews are not "real" to her. But there is another interpretation. The trouble with the Prioress's conception of Jews, as David correctly points out and as I have noted earlier in this essay, is precisely that it ignores historical reality. As long as wicked Jews live exclusively in a childish imagination, and there is no actual contact with real Jews, the practical harm may be minimal, whatever the injury to truth, whatever the moral culpability. But when carriers of such childish distortions meet real Jews (or blacks, or professors, or business tycoons, or any other stereotypes) for the first time in the flesh, how do they react? While we cannot know for sure what was in Chaucer's mind when he gave the Prioress these anti-Semitic prejudices, we do know that, from his earlier minor narrative poems through the creation of the Wife of Bath, Chaucer was very interested in the relationship between authority (whether literary or ecclesiastical) and experience. And while Chaucer's poetry displays a love of books and reverence for Christianity, this practical man of affairs also shows immense respect for the value of experience.

To see the anti-Semitism of *The Prioress's Tale* as I have tried to suggest here is not to conclude, as Friedman claims critics of the Prioress do conclude, that she is a "malicious, cruel-minded bigot." Chaucer is subtler than that, and the moral meaning of the Prioress and her Tale is more interesting than that. D.W. Robertson, Jr, supporting his argument with extensive references to medieval sculpture and manuscript illumination, warns us not to read medieval fictional characters exactly as we would those of modern times, namely, as if they were representational individuals. Robertson does not deny "realistic" elements in Chaucer; he notes the poet's "tendency to mingle details of an iconographic nature with other details which produce an effect of considerable verisimilitude." But he puts that verisimilitude into a larger historical context: "although the characters in the Prologue have an undeniable verisimilitude, consistent with increasing interest in verisimilitude in the visual arts, they are in no sense 'realistic.' The function of the verisimilitude is, first of all, to attract attention, and ultimately, to show the validity of the underlying abstractions as they manifest themselves in the life of the times."[28] Robertson specifically applies this notion of medieval characterization to his analysis of the Prioress and the other pilgrims in the General Prologue. Following Roberton's lead, we may view the Prioress not in the main as an imitation of an actual fourteenth-century person but rather as an illustration of a set of attitudes, values, and traditions. She stands, in part, for innocence and the pernicious consequences that may result from that condition.

In his comment on *The Prioress's Tale* John Gardner writes, "Innocence doesn't necessarily (as Henry James kept noticing) make virtue."[29] Chaucer, I think, goes further. Through the Prioress, her pious miracle of the Virgin, and the virulent anti-Semitism in it, Chaucer deftly exposes the danger of innocence. Two and a half centuries before Milton, the bookish but worldly Chaucer showed that he also would not praise a "fugitive and cloistered virtue."

CHAPTER TWO

Shylock and the Idea of the Jew

DEREK COHEN

Shylock is the best-known Jew in English. In the eighteenth, nineteenth, and twentieth centuries, Shylock's name enters the language as a term of abuse. The memorable Jews of English literature discussed in this volume − Fagin, Riah, Melmotte, and even Daniel Deronda and Leopold Bloom − are in some way either elaborations of Shylock or responses to him. Shylock is the formidable measure of them all. What Shylock means thus becomes crucial to all English writing that deals with the Jewish presence. The Jewish presence in English literature takes its form from Shylock. Allen Koretsky has scrutinized Chaucer for the presence of evil embodied in mythical Jews. But Shylock is the humanization of the Jew; Shylock, as he notoriously reminds us, has blood and bones and tears and laughter.

The Merchant of Venice endures: Shylock endures as a man and a monster. But the ambiguity of the play has produced the frustration which has spawned the debate about what Shylock is and what he represents. This debate has usually taken place between inexpert Jewish readers and spectators, who discern the play's anti-Semitism, and literary critics (many of them Jews) who defensively maintain that Shakespeare's subtlety of mind transcends anti-Semitism. The critics' arguments, by now familiar, centre on the subject of Shylock's essential humanity, point to the imperfections of the Christians, and remind us that Shakespeare was writing in a period when there were so few Jews in England that it didn't matter anyway (or, alternatively, that because there were so few Jews in England, Shakespeare had probably never met one, so he didn't really know what he was doing). Where I believe the defensive arguments go wrong is in their heavy concentration on the character of Shylock; they overlook the play's attempt to offer a total poetic image of the Jew.

It is all very well for John Russell Brown to say *The Merchant of Venice* is not anti-Jewish, and that "there are only two slurs on Jews in general"[1]; but this kind of assertion, though common in criticism of the play, cannot account for the fear and shame that Jewish viewers and readers have often felt from the moment of Shylock's entrance on stage to his final exit. I wish to argue that these feelings are justified and that such an intuitive response is as valid as the critical sophistries whose purpose is to exonerate Shakespeare from the charge of anti-Semitism. Although few writers on the subject are prepared to concede as much, it is quite possible that Shakespeare didn't give a damn about Jews or about insulting England's minuscule Jewish community, and that, if he did finally humanize his Jew, he did so simply to enrich his drama. We can, of course, never know. The kind of reading, so thoroughly embedded in the cultural system which produced plays like *The Merchant of Venice*, validates the search for a monological, single meaning of a literary work. Shakespeare criticism has been dominated by the impulse to discover the meaning of a work largely by the search to discover what the "author" meant. A reasoned argument can demonstrate that Shakespeare meant it this way or that. The play is or is not a vehicle that demonizes the Jew because this is how the author meant it. *The Merchant of Venice* possesses and uses ugly racial stereotyping and also it does the other: it challenges and subverts such stereotyping.

In this chapter I wish to demonstrate that *The Merchant of Venice* is an anti-Semitic play by examining the image of Jewishness that it presents and by placing that image in the contrasting context of Christianity to which it is automatically made referable. I also wish to examine the paradox that follows from my assertion of the anti-Semitic nature of the play – that is, the paradox of Shylock's humanization in his final scene when he is made simultaneously the villain of the drama and its unfortunate victim.

Let us first ask what is meant by anti-Semitism when that term is applied to a work of art. Leo Kirschbaum suggests that it is a "wholly irrational prejudice against Jews in general," noting it would be difficult to accuse any of the Christian characters in *The Merchant of Venice* of such a vice.[2] This seems to be John Russell Brown's view as well; he perceives the play's only anti-Semitic remarks to be Launcelot's statement "my master's a very

Jew" (II, ii, 100) and Antonio's comment about Shylock's "Jewish heart" (IV, i, 80). [3] While generally acceptable, Kirschbaum's definition seems to err in its use of the term "irrational." Prejudice is almost always rationalized; it is rationalized by reference to history and mythology. Jews have been hated for a number of reasons, the most potent among them that the Jews were the killers of Jesus Christ.

I would define an anti-Semitic work of art as one that portrays Jews in a way that makes them objects of antipathy to readers and spectators – objects of scorn, hatred, laughter, or contempt. A careful balance is needed to advance this definition, since it might seem to preclude the possibility of an artist's presenting any Jewish character in negative terms without incurring the charge of anti-Semitism. Obviously, Jews must be allowed to have their faults in art as they do in life. In my view, a work of art becomes anti-Semitic not by virtue of its portrayal of an individual Jew in uncomplimentary terms but by its association of negative racial characteristics with the term Jewish or with Jewish characters generally. What we must do, then, is look at the way the word Jew is used and how Jews are portrayed in *The Merchant of Venice* as a whole.

The word *Jew* is used fifty-eight times in *The Merchant of Venice*. Variants of the word like *Jewess*, *Jew's*, and *Jewish* are used fourteen times; *Hebrew* is used twice. There are, then, seventy-four direct uses of Jew and unambiguously related words in the play. Since it can readily be acknowledged that Shakespeare understood the dramatic and rhetorical power of iteration, it must follow that there is a deliberate reason for the frequency of the use of the word in the play. And as in all of Shakespeare's plays, that reason is to surround and inform the term with associations which, as it is used, come more and more easily to mind. A word apparently used neutrally in the early moments of a play gains significance as it is repeated; it becomes a term with connotations that infuse it with additional meaning.

The word *Jew* has no neutral connotations in drama. Unlike, say, the word *blood* as it is used in *Richard II* or *Macbeth* – where the connotations deepen in proportion not merely to the frequency with which the word is uttered but to the poetic significance of the passages in which it is employed – *Jew* has strongly negative implications in *The Merchant of Venice*. It is surely significant that Shylock is addressed as "Shylock" only seventeen times in the play. On all other occasions he is called "Jew" and is referred to as "the Jew." Even when he and Antonio are presumed to be on an equal footing, Shylock is referred to as the Jew while Antonio is referred to by name. For example, in the putatively disinterested letter written by the learned doctor Bellario to commend Balthazar/Portia, there is the phrase "*I acquainted him with the cause in controversy between the Jew and Antonio*" (IV, i, 154–6).[4] Similarly, in the court scene, Portia calls Shylock by his name only twice; for the rest of the scene she calls him "Jew" to his face. The reason for this is, of course, to set Shylock apart from the other characters, to discriminate against him. This it does successfully. Calling the villain of the play by a name which generalizes him and at the same time ostensibly defines his essence acts, in a sense, to depersonalize him. As in our own daily life, where terms such as *bourgeois*, *communist*, and *fascist* conveniently efface the humanness and individuality of those to whom they are applied, the constant reference to Shylock's "thingness" succeeds in depriving him of his humanity while simultaneously justifying the hostility of his enemies. The word *Jew* has long conjured up associations of foreignness in the minds of non-Jews. When it is used repeatedly to refer to the bloodthirsty villain of *The Merchant of Venice*, its intention is unmistakable. And the more often it is used in the play, the more difficult it is for the audience to see it as a neutral word. Even if John Russell Brown is correct in pointing out that there are only two overtly anti-Semitic uses of the word in the play, it can surely be acknowledged that overt anti-Semitic references are unnecessary after the early scenes in the play. Each time that *Jew* is used by any of Shylock's enemies, the deeply anti-Jewish implication is automatically assumed.

In act I, scene iii, after the bond has been struck, Antonio turns to the departing Shylock and murmurs "Hie thee gentle Jew. / The Hebrew will turn Christian, he grows kind" (ll. 177–8). The lines themselves seem inoffensive, but let us examine the words and the gestures they imply. Shylock has left the stage and Antonio is commenting on the bond that has just been sealed. It is impossible to ignore the mocking tone of Antonio's words and the fact that the scorn they express is directed toward Shylock's Jewishness as much as toward Shylock himself. Surely, too, the elevation of one religion over another is accomplished only if one of those religions is deemed inferior. To imply that Shylock is so improved (however ironically this is meant) that he verges on becoming Christian is an expression of amused superiority to Jews. The relatively mild anti-Semitism implicit in this passage is significant because it is so common in the play and because it leads with the inexorable logic of historical truth to the more fierce and destructive kind of anti-Semitism. While Shylock the Jew is still regarded as a nasty but harmless smudge on the landscape, he is grudgingly accorded some human potential by the Christians; once he becomes a threat to their happiness, however, the quality in him which is initially disdained — his Jewishness — becomes the very cynosure of fear and loathing.

In its early stages, for example, the play makes only lighthearted connections between the Jew and the devil: as the connections are validated over and over again by Shylock's behaviour, they become charged with meaning. When Launcelot is caught in the contortions of debating with himself the pros and cons of leaving Shylock's service, he gives the association of Jew and devil clear expression: "Certainly, my conscience will serve me to run from this Jew my master ... To be rul'd by my conscience, I should stay with the Jew my master, who (God bless the mark) is a kind of devil; and to run away from the Jew, I should be rul'd by the fiend, who, saving your reverence, is the devil himself. Certainly the Jew is the very devil incarnation, and in my conscience, my conscience is but a kind of hard conscience, to offer to counsel me to stay with the Jew" (II, ii, 1–30). Significant here is the almost obsessive repetition of "the Jew." In the immediate context the phrase has a neat dramatic ambiguity; it refers explicitly to Shylock but, by avoiding the use of his name, it also refers more generally to the concept of the Jew. The ambiguity of the phrase makes the demonic association applicable to Jews generally.

That Launcelot's description is anti-Jewish more than simply anti-Shylock is to be seen in the fact that the view of the Jew it presents, which is in accord with the anti-Semitic portrayal of Jews dating from the Middle Ages. Launcelot's image of the Jew as the devil incarnate conforms to a common medieval notion. It is expressed in Chaucer and much early English drama, and it is given powerful theological support by Luther, who warns the Christian world that "next to the devil thou hast no enemy more cruel, more venomous and violent than a true Jew."[5] That a fool like Launcelot should take the assertion a step further and see the Jew as the devil himself is only to be expected. And that the play should show, finally, that Shylock is only a devil *manqué* lends further support to Luther's influential asseveration.

A less mythological but more colourful and dramatically effective anti-Jewish association is forged by the frequent and almost casually employed metaphor of Jew as dog. The play is replete with dialogue describing Shylock in these terms. In the mouth of Solanio, for example, the connection is explicit: "I never heard a passion so confus'd, / So strange, outrageous and so variable / As the dog Jew did utter in the streets" (II, viii, 12–14). I do not believe that it is going too far to suggest that in this passage the word *strange* carried a host of anti-Semitic reverberations. To the traditional anti-Semitic memory it recalls something foreign, and, to the ignorant, it recalls frightening Jewish rituals of mourning – rituals which in anti-Semitic literature were redolent with implications of the slaughter of Christian children and the drinking of their blood. This report of Shylock's rage and grief marks a massive turning point in the play. The once verminous Jew is implicitly transformed into a fearful force.

To this argument I must add a point about a passage rarely discussed in the critical literature on the play. Having bemoaned his losses and decided to take his revenge, Shylock turns to Tubal and tells him to get an officer to arrest Antonio. "I will have the heart of him if he forfeit, for were he out of Venice I can make what merchandise I will. Go, Tubal," he says, "and meet me at our synagogue; go good Tubal, at our synagogue, Tubal" (III, i, 127–30). This collusive and sinister request to meet at the synagogue has always seemed to me to be the most deeply anti-Semitic remark in the play. It is pernicious precisely because it is indirect. What is the word *synagogue* supposed to mean in the context? Shylock has just determined to cut the heart out of the finest man in Venice; worse yet, the knowledge that he is legally entitled to do so brings him solace in his grief. Now what might an Elizabethan have thought the synagogue really was? Is it possible that he thought it merely a place where Jews prayed? Is it not more likely that he thought it a mysterious place where strange and terrible rituals were enacted? Whatever Shakespeare himself might have thought, the lines convey the notion that Shylock is repairing to his place of worship immediately after learning that he can now legally murder the good Antonio. Bloodletting and religious worship are brought into a very ugly and insidious conjunction.

Earlier, Tubal is observed approaching Solanio, who remarks, "Here comes another of the tribe; a third cannot be match'd, unless the devil himself turn Jew" (III, i, 76–7). Incredible as it may seem, this line has been used to demonstrate that the play is not anti-Semitic, because Shylock and Tubal alone among the Jews are so bad as to be like devils. What the lines as strongly propose is that these two villains are the worst Jews around, and that as the worst of a very bad lot they must be pretty bad.

In her study of the origins of modern German anti-Semitism, Lucy Dawidowicz discerns two irreconcilable images of Jews in anti-Semitic literature "both inherited from the recent and medieval treasury of anti-Semitism. One was the image of the Jew as vermin, to be rubbed out by the heel of the boot, to be exterminated. The other was the image of the Jew as the mythic omnipotent superadversary, against whom war on the greatest scale had to be conducted. The Jew was, on the one hand, a germ, a bacillus, to be killed without conscience. On the other hand, he was, in the phrase Hitler repeatedly used ... the 'mortal enemy' (*Todfiend*) to be killed in self-defense."[6] The Christians in *The Merchant of Venice* initially see Shylock in terms of the first image. He is a dog to be spurned and spat upon. His Jewish gaberdine and his Jewish habits of usury mark him as a cur to be kicked. (Is it likely that Antonio would enjoy the same license to kick a rich Christian moneylender with impunity?) As Shylock gains in power, however, his image as a cur changes to that of a potent diabolical force. In Antonio's eyes Shylock's lust for blood takes on the motive energy of Satanic evil, impervious to reason or humanity.

> I pray you think you question with the Jew:
> You may as well go stand upon the beach
> And bid the main flood bate his usual height;
> You may as well use question with the wolf
> Why he hath made the ewe bleak for the lamb;
> You may as well forbid the mountain pines
> To wag their high tops, and to make no noise
> When they are fretten with the gusts of heaven;
> You may as well do anything most hard
> As seek to soften that – than which what's harder? –
> His Jewish heart! (IV, i, 70–80)

In this speech Shylock is utterly "the Jew" – the embodiment of his species. And the Jew's Jewish heart is wholly obdurate. He is a force of evil as strong as nature itself. No longer a dog to be controlled by beating and kicking, he has become an untamable wolf, an inferno of evil and hatred. The logical conclusion of sentiments like these, surely, is that the Jew must be kept down. Once he is up, his instinct is to kill and ravage.

Indeed, Shylock has said as much himself: "Thou call'dst me dog before thou hadst a cause, / But since I am a dog, beware my fangs" (III, iii, 6–7). If the play defines Christianity as synonymous with tolerance and kindness and forgiveness, it defines Jewishness in opposite terms. The symbol of evil in *The Merchant of Venice* is Jewishness, and Jewishness is represented by the Jew.

The counterargument to the charge that Shakespeare is guilty of anti-Semitism has always depended upon the demonstration that the portrait of Shylock is, ultimately, a deeply humane one – that Shylock's arguments against the Christians are unassailable and that his position in the Christian world has resulted from that world's treatment of him. This view, Romantic in inception, still persists in the minds of a large number of critics and theatre directors. From such authors as John Palmer and Harold Goddard one gets the image of a Shylock who carried with him the Jewish heritage of suffering and persecution, Shylock as bearer of the pain of the ages. This Shylock is religious and dignified, wronged by the world he inhabits, a man of whom the Jewish people can justly be proud and in whose vengeful intentions they may recognize a poetic righting of the wrongs of Jewish history.[7] That Jews have themselves recognized such a Shylock in Shakespeare's play is borne out in the self-conscious effusions of Heinrich Heine, for whom the Jewish moneylender possessed "a breast that held in it all the martyrdom ... [of] a whole tortured people."[8]

The usual alternative to this view is that of the critics who see Shylock as no more than a stereotyped villain. For them, what his sympathizers regard as a plea for Shylock's essential humanity (the "Hath not a Jew eyes" speech [II, i, 59 ff.]) is nothing more than a justification for revenge. These critics circumvent the charge that the text is anti-Semitic by arguing that Shylock is not so much a Jew as a carryover from the old morality plays. Albert Wertheim, for example, asserts that "Shylock is a stylized and conventional comic villain and is no more meant to be a realistic portrayal of a Jew than Shakespeare's Aaron is meant to be a realistic Moor."[9] John P. Sisk confidently declares that "Kittredge was mainly right in his contention that the play is not an anti-Semitic document."[10] These views, which are determinedly anti-sentimental, balance the oversensitive opposing position. They argue dramatic precedent on the basis of the similarities between Shylock and the stereotypical comic villain of earlier dramatic modes. Toby Lelyveld notes striking resemblances between Shylock and the Pantalone figures of *commedia dell'arte*, for example, "In physical appearance, mannerisms and the situations in which he is placed, Shylock is so like his Italian prototype that his characterization, at least superficially, presents no new aspects save that of its Jewishness."[11]

What the two critical opinions have in common is their determination to defend Shakespeare from the charge of anti-Semitism − but they do so from opposite sides of the fence. Shylock is either a better man than we might be disposed to believe, or he is not really human.[12] Though it is possible that Shakespeare intended both readings, it is undoubtedly true that Shylock's "humanity" has often been given full, even excessive, play in the theatre. But it is always useful to bear in mind that he is the play's villain. All his words, even the most convincingly aggrieved among them, are the words of a would-be killer, and might therefore be regarded skeptically. Shylock is untouched by the plight of those around him, and he plots the ruthless murder of Antonio. Pity for him therefore strikes me as grossly misplaced, and the view of him as the embodiment of wickedness seems viable dramatically. His arguments that he is like other men and that he is vengeful only because he has been wronged by them is a violent corruption of the true state of things. Shylock is cruel and monstrous and utterly unlike other men in their capacity for love, fellowship, and sympathy. Consider his remark that he would not have exchanged the ring his daughter stole for a "wilderness of monkeys." It does not redeem him, as Kirschbaum points out, but makes him worse; by demonstrating that he is capable of sentiment and aware of love, the remark "blackens by contrast his inhumanity all the more."[13] In any case the line is out of character. It is the only reference to Shylock's wife in the play, and, if we are to take his treatment of Jessica as an indication of his treatment of those he professes to hold dear, we may reasonably conclude that it is an expression not necessarily of love but of sentimental self-pity − though it needs to be said that the moment of this expression is fraught with potential complexity for the thoughtful reader. Shylock is, according to this reading, however, a complete and unredeemed villain whose wickedness is a primary trait. It is a trait, moreover, that is reinforced by the fact of his Jewishness, which, to make the wickedness so much the worse, is presented as synonymous with it.

And yet, although Shylock is the villain of the play, the critics who have been made uneasy by the characterization of his evil have also sensed a dimension of pathos, a quality of humanity. Audiences and readers have usually found themselves pitying Shylock in the end, even though the play's other characters, having demolished him, hardly give the wicked Jew a second thought. These Christians fail to see the humanity of Shylock not because they are less sensitive than readers and spectators but because that humanity emerges chiefly in the end, during the court scene when the characters are caught up in the atmosphere of happiness surrounding Antonio's release from death. Audiences and readers, whose attention is likely to be given equally to Antonio and Shylock, are more aware of what is happening to Shylock. They are therefore aware of the change that is forced upon him. To them he is more than simply an undone villain. He is capable of suffering, and therefore, surprisingly, capable of inhabiting what our culture teaches us is the highest of all realms, that of tragedy.

Shylock becomes a pitiable character during his last appearance in the court of Venice. It is here that he is humanized — during a scene in which he is usually silent. Ironically, it is not in his pleadings or self-justifications that Shylock becomes a sympathetic figure, but in his still and silent transformation from a crowing, blood-hungry monster into a quiescent victim whose fate lies in the hands of those he had attempted to destroy. How this transmogrification is accomplished is, perhaps, best explained by Gordon Craig's exquisitely simple observation about the chief character of *The Bells*: "no matter who the human being may be, and what his crime, the sorrow which he suffers must appeal to our hearts"[14]. This observation helps explain why the scene of reversal that turns aside the impending catastrophe of *The Merchant of Venice* does not leave the audience with feelings of unmixed delight as do the reversals of more conventional comedies. The reversal of *The Merchant of Venice* defies a basic premise of the normal moral logic of drama. Instead of merely enjoying the overthrow of an unmitigated villain, we find ourselves pitying him. The conclusion of the play is thus a triumph of ambiguity: Shakespeare has sustained the moral argument which dictates Shylock's undoing while simultaneously compelling us to react on a level that is more compassionate than intellectual.

If it is true that Jewishness in the play is equated with wickedness, it is unlikely that Shylock's elaborate rationalizations of his behaviour are intended to render him as sympathetic. Embedded in the lengthy speeches of self-justification are statements that reflect Shylock's motives more accurately than the passages in which he identifies himself as wrongly and malevolently persecuted. In his first encounter with Antonio, for example, Shylock explains in a deeply felt aside why he hates the Christian merchant: "I hate him for he is a Christian; / But more, for that in low simplicity / He lends out money gratis, and brings down / The rate of usance here with us in Venice" (I, iii, 42–5). It is only as an afterthought that he ponders the larger question of Antonio's hatred of the Jews. Shylock announces that his chief reason for hating Antonio relates directly to Antonio's avarice in money matters.

Almost all of Shylock's speeches can be convincingly interpreted in this light. When he speaks, Shylock is a sarcastic character both in the literal sense of flesh-rending and in the modern sense of sneering. For example, when he describes the bloody agreement as a "merry bond," the word *merry* is charged with a sinister ambiguity. Until the scene of his undoing, Shylock's character is dominated by the traits usual to Elizabethan comic villains. He is a hellish creature, a discontented soul whose vilifying of others marks him as the embodiment of malevolence and misanthropy. After Jessica's escape Shylock is seen vituperating his daughter, not mourning her, bemoaning the loss of his money as much as the loss of his child. His affirmations of his common humanity with the Christians, particularly in the "Hath not a Jew eyes" speech, are above all meant to justify his thirst for revenge. His allegations that Antonio has disgraced him, laughed at him, and scorned his nation only because he is a Jew are lopsided. He is abused chiefly because he is a devil. The fact of his Jewishness offers his abusers an explanation for his diabolical nature; it does not offer them the pretext to torment an innocent man. His speech of wheedling self-exculpation is surely intended to be regarded in the way that beleaguered tenants today might regard the whine of their wealthy landlord: "Hath not a landlord eyes? Hath not a landlord organs, dimensions, senses, affections, passions?" Instead of eliciting sympathy for an underdog, Shakespeare seems to have intended the speech to elicit detestation for one in a privileged and powerful position who knowingly and deliberately abases himself in a plea for unmerited sympathy.

In answer to the tradition that defends Shylock on the grounds that Shakespeare gave him a sympathetic, self-protecting speech, let us be reminded that its assertions are dependent upon a demonstrable falsehood. The climax of Shylock's speech, its cutting edge, is his confident cry that his revenge is justified by Christian precedent: "If a Jew wrong a Christian, what is his humility? Revenge. If a Christian wrong a Jew, what should his sufferance be by Christian example? Why, revenge" (III, i, 68–71). Yet in return for the crime which Shylock commits against Antonio, Shylock is offered not revenge but mercy – harshly given perhaps, but mercy nonetheless – and this in circumstances where revenge would be morally and legally sanctioned. The director who causes this speech to be uttered as a genuine defence of its speaker is thus ignoring one of the play's most tangible morals.

Until the court scene, Shylock remains for the most part a readily understood and easily identified villain. His dominant characteristics are the negative qualities normally associated with vice figures. Being completely in the ascendancy, he has power and the law on his side. When sympathy for Shylock finally becomes right and proper, it transcends the narrow bounds of religion and stereotype. When, finally, we are made to pity Shylock, we do not pity a wrongfully persecuted member of an oppressed minority but a justly condemned and justly punished villain. A potential murderer has been caught, is brought to justice, and is duly and appropriately sentenced. The pity we are moved to feel is as natural and inevitable as the great loathing we were formerly made to feel. Pity results from the sympathy one is likely to admit at any sight of human suffering, no matter how well deserved it may be.

In the court scene Portia's presence is a direct indication that Antonio will not die. While we remain conscious of Shylock's evil intentions, our judgment of him is tempered by our privileged awareness of his ultimate impotence. In other words, although we might despise Shylock, we do not fear him. This distinction is critical to an understanding of his character and of Shakespeare's intentions, and it helps explain the readiness with which we are able to extend sympathy to the villain.

The chief explanation, however, goes somewhat deeper. It is simultaneously psychological and dramatic: psychological to the extent that we are willy-nilly affected by the sight of Shylock in pain; dramatic to the extent that the scene is so arranged as to dramatize in the subtlest way the manifestation of that pain.

Shylock remains onstage while his erstwhile victims are re-
stored to prosperity by Portia. The publication of Antonio's rescue and of Shylock's punishment takes ninety-six lines, from
Portia's "Tarry a little, there is something else" (IV, i, 305) to
Gratiano's gleeful "Had I been judge, thou shouldst have had
ten more, / To bring thee to the gallows, not to the font" (399–
400). During this time – about five minutes – Shylock is transformed from a villain into a victim.

In part the inversion is achieved by use of the established fool,
Gratiano. By trumpeting the victory of the Christians, he as-
sumes Shylock's earlier role as one who enjoys another's pain.
Gratiano is a character who talks too much, who suspects silence, who prefers to play the fool. His joy in Shylock's downfall
becomes sadistic and self-serving. Interestingly, Gratiano's joy
is not shared in quite so voluble a fashion by the other Christian
characters. Portia has done all the work, and yet it is Gratiano
– whose real contribution to the scene is to announce Portia's
success and to excoriate the Jew – who cries at Shylock "Now,
infidel, I have you on the hip" (334). Until this point in the play
Shylock has been vicious and sadistic, nastily rubbing his hands
in anticipation of a bloody revenge, thriving on the smell of the
blood he is about to taste. Now that role is taken from him by
Gratiano, on whom it sits unattractively. The failure of Gratiano's friends to participate in this orgy of revenge suggests
that their feelings are more those of relief at Antonio's release
than of lust for Shylock's blood.

As the tables are turned upon him, Shylock gradually and
unexpectedly reveals a new dimension of himself, and the far-
cical pleasure we have been led to expect is subverted by his
surprising response to defeat. He reveals a capacity for pain
and suffering. As a would-be murderer, Shylock gets at least
what he deserves. As a human being asking for mercy, he receives, and possibly merits, sympathy. Shylock recognizes instantly that he has been undone. Once Portia reminds him that
the bond does not allow him to shed one drop of blood, his orgy
is over and he says little during the scene of *dénouement*. "Is
that the law?" (315) he lamely asks. Five lines later, he is ready
to take his money and leave the court with whatever dignity is
permitted him. But his egress is not to be easy; he is made to
face the consequences of his evil. Portia's addresses to Shylock
during the confrontation are disguised exhortations to him to
suffer for the wrong he has done. She forces him to acknowledge
her triumph and his defeat: "Tarry a little" (305); "Soft ... soft,

no haste!" (320–1); "Why doth the Jew pause?" (335); "Therefore prepare thee to cut" (324); "Tarry Jew" (346); "Art thou contented, Jew? what dost thou say?" (393). Shylock is made to stand silently, receiving and accepting mercy and some restitution from Antonio; he is compelled to bear not the stings of revenge upon himself but the sharper stings of a forgiveness that he is incapable of giving. His humiliation lies in his inability to refuse the gift of life from one whose life he maliciously sought. When he requests leave to go from the court, the change that has come over him is total. He is no longer a figure of vice, and he has not become a figure of fun (except, perhaps, to Gratiano). He is a lonely, deprived, and defeated creature who feels pain. The fact that he has caused his own downfall does not diminish our sympathy, in part because of the protraction of his undoing, and in part because of the dramatic effect of the change in him. The suddenness of the alteration of his character forces a comparison between what he once was and what he has become. And where dramatic energy is its own virtue, the visible eradication of the energy is a source of pathos.

In this scene the word *Jew* is used like a blunt instrument by Portia and Gratiano. Now used against one who has become a victim, the word's former associations are thrown into question. Portia's persistence in doing to the Jew as he would have done to Antonio has a strangely bitter effect. She hunts him when he is down; she throws the law in his teeth with a righteousness that seems repulsive to us primarily because we have long been aware that Antonio was ultimately invulnerable. Having removed Shylock's sting, she is determined to break his wings in the bargain. In this she is unlike her somewhat dull but more humane husband, who is prepared to pay Shylock the money owed him and to allow him to leave. Portia's stance is beyond legal questioning, of course. What gives us pause is the doggedness with which she exacts justice. Shylock is ruined by adversity and leaves the stage without even the strength to curse his foes: "I pray you give me leave to go from hence, / I am not well" (395–6). He communicates his pain by his powerlessness, and the recognition of this pain stirs the audience.

In a brief space, in which his silence replaces his usual verbosity, Shylock is transformed. A villain is shown to be more than merely villainous. Shylock is shown to be more than merely the Jew. He is shown to possess a normal, unheroic desire to live at any cost. This scene of undoing makes Shylock's previously histrionic pleas for understanding all the more ironic. We now see something that formerly there was no reason to believe: that if you prick him, Shylock bleeds.

By endowing Shylock with humanity in the end, Shakespeare would seem to have contradicted the dominant impression of the play, that of the fierce diabolism of the Jew. Having described a character who is defined by an almost otherworldly evil, whose life is one unremitting quest for an unjust vengeance, it seems inconsistent to allow that he is capable of normal human feelings. The Jew has been used to instruct the audience and the Christians of the play about the potential and essential evil of his race; he has been used to show that a Jew with power is a terrible thing to behold, is capable of the vilest sort of destruction. And the play has demonstrated in the person of his daughter that the only good Jew is a Christian. The contradiction emerges almost in spite of Shakespeare's apparent anti-Semitic design. He has shown on the one hand, by the creation of a powerful and dominant dramatic image, that the Jew is inhuman. But he seems to have been compelled on the other hand to acknowledge that the Jew is also a human being.

The most troubling aspect of the contradictory element of *The Merchant of Venice* is this: if Shakespeare knew that Jews were human beings like other people – and the conclusion of the play suggests that he did – and if he knew that they were not *merely* carriers of evil but human creatures with human strengths and weaknesses, then the play as a whole is a betrayal of the truth. That Shakespeare used the play to elicit feelings of loathing for Jews, while simultaneously recognizing that its portrayal was inaccurate or, possibly, not the whole truth, is profoundly troubling. It is as though *The Merchant of Venice* is an anti-Semitic play written by an author who is not an anti-Semite – but an author who has been willing to use the cruel stereotypes of that ideology for mercenary and artistic purposes.

The Outcast as Villain and Victim: Jews in Dickens's Oliver Twist and Our Mutual Friend

DEBORAH HELLER

There are peripheral Jewish characters in several of Dickens's novels, but Jews play important roles in only two of them. In *Oliver Twist*, his second novel (1837–39), Dickens created his most famous Jewish character, Fagin, a diabolical "fence" who is the systematic exploiter of childhood innocence. Almost thirty years later, in his thirteenth and last completed novel, *Our Mutual Friend* (1864–65), Dickens created the less widely known and dramatically less successful Jewish character, Mr Riah. In contrast to Fagin, Riah appears as a wholly virtuous, patriarchal figure, the friend and protector of neglected, menaced, innocent children. Whether as the incarnation of Vice or of Virtue, however, the two most important Jews in Dickens's work are defined in the context of the conflict between innocence and worldly evil. In this conflict, which preoccupied Dickens throughout his fiction, innocence re-emerges time and again as menaced or exploited childhood; evil, on the other hand, appears in many guises, wearing various – and changing – faces. An examination of Fagin and Mr Riah, the embodiments of opposing Jewish stereotypes, may possibly reveal something of Dickens's shifting attitudes toward Jews; it will certainly help us chart the changing face of evil in his world.

Fagin ranks second only to Shylock as one of the most memorable – and infamous – Jews in all of English literature. He is a fence, that is, a receiver of stolen goods, and he has in his employ a group of children and young adults whom he has educated to thievery and prostitution while posing as their protector. The children, who are all homeless orphans (as is Oliver), live with Fagin in his house. It is a kind of boarding school offering instruction in crime, though its gaiety is more characteristic of a summer camp. Fagin's evil is directly related to his financial unscrupulousness, as is traditional in the negative stereotype of the Jew with which Dickens and his readers were familiar. Fagin embodies many characteristics long associated with Jews in English literature, particularly dramatic literature: he is dishonest, thieving, treacherous, avaricious, and ultimately cowardly. Moreover, he is not only a thief but, indirectly, a murderer as well. He arranges for the capture and execution of those members of his gang who have outlived their usefulness and are dangerous to him. Fagin also incites Bill Sikes to the climactic murder of Nancy, after failing in his efforts to incite Nancy to poison Sikes.

In later years Dickens was to deny that there had been any anti-Semitic intent behind the creation of his Jewish villain. In 1854, "the *Jewish Chronicle* had asked 'why Jews alone should be excluded from the sympathizing heart' of this great author and powerful friend of the oppressed." Dickens responded in reply to an invitation to an anniversary dinner of the Westminster Jewish Free School, "I know of no reason the Jews can have for regarding me as 'inimical' to them." He then cited the sympathetic way in which he had treated the persecution of the Jews in his *Child's History of England* (1851). "On the contrary," he wrote, "I believe I do my part toward the assertion of their civil and religious liberty, and in my *Child's History of England* I have expressed a strong abhorrence of their persecution in old time."[1]

Nine years later, in 1863, Dickens entered into an interesting correspondence with Mrs Eliza Davis, who, with her husband James, a banker, had bought Dickens's London home, Tavistock House, three years earlier. Though excerpts from this correspondence have been widely cited elsewhere, it offers such a valuable point of departure for considering the Jewishness of Dickens's first villain that it would seem foolish not to consider it here as well. The Davises were Jewish, and, in a letter to Dickens, Mrs Davis gave voice to the distress of Dickens's Jewish readership: "It has been said that Charles Dickens, the large-hearted, whose works plead so eloquently and so nobly for the oppressed of this country ... has encouraged a vile prejudice against the despised Hebrew ... Fagin I fear admits only of one interpretation; but (while) Charles Dickens lives the author can justify himself or atone for a great wrong."[2]

Dickens's answer reads in part:

if there be any general feeling on the part of the intelligent Jewish
people, that I have done them what you describe as "a great wrong,"
they are a far less sensible, a far less just, and a far less good-tempered
people than I have always supposed them to be. Fagin, in *Oliver Twist*,
is a Jew, because it unfortunately was true of the time to which that
story refers, that that class of criminal almost invariably was a Jew.
But surely no sensible man or woman of your persuasion can fail to
observe – firstly, that all the rest of the wicked *dramatis personae* are
Christians; and secondly, that he is called a "Jew," not because of his
religion, but because of his race. If I were to write a story, in which I
described a Frenchman or a Spaniard as "the Roman Catholic," I should
do a very indecent and unjustifiable thing; but I make mention of Fagin
as the Jew, because he is one of the Jewish people, and because it
conveys that kind of idea of him which I should give my readers of a
Chinaman, by calling him a Chinese.

A most curious disclaimer of anti-Jewish intent on Dickens's
part. Indeed, it seems to me impossible to treat Dickens's response to Mrs Davis' objections with the credulity he demands.
Mrs Davis herself did not, for she replied: "It is a fact that the
Jewish *race* and *religion* are inseparable, if a Jew embrace any
other faith, he is no longer known as one of the *race* either to
his own people or to the Gentiles to whom he has joined himself
… If, as you remark 'all must observe that the other Criminals
were Christians' they are at least contrasted with characters of
good Christians, this poor wretched Fagin stands alone 'The
Jew.'" This letter also contained a suggestion that is generally
credited with providing Dickens the impetus for creating his
good Jew, Mr Riah, in *Our Mutual Friend*, written a year or so
later. "I hazard the opinion," Mrs Davis wrote, "that it would
well repay an author of reputation to examine more closely into
the manners and characters of the British Jews and to represent
them as they really are."

It seems clear that by the time of the exchange with Mrs Davis
in 1863, and his writing of *Our Mutual Friend* starting in 1864,
Dickens definitely did not wish to be thought of as anti-Semitic
or hostile to Jews. His rationalization of Fagin's Jewishness as
incidental to his role in *Oliver Twist*, as a kind of historical
accident ("because it unfortunately was true of the time to which
that story refers, that that class of criminal almost invariably
was a Jew"), may have represented a sincere attempt to convince

himself of what he would have liked to believe was true. It well may be, too, that Dickens's personal views of Jews had undergone something of a shift between his creation of Fagin and his much later defence of that creation, a matter we shall return to shortly. For the moment, however, I should like to examine the justice of Mrs Davis' original objection, "Fagin I fear admits of only one interpretation."

The claim that Fagin's Jewishness is somehow incidental to his conception, that it is a kind of historical accident, would be almost too preposterous to take seriously had it not been advanced by Dickens himself and treated seriously by many critics since his time.[3] However, the fact remains that Dickens chose to stress unremittingly Fagin's Jewishness. One cannot but be struck by the persistence with which Fagin is referred to throughout the novel as "the Jew." If Dickens – or any other writer – were consistently to refer to a villain as "the Frenchman" or "the Chinaman," no reader could be faulted for supposing the writer was making a considered point about the generic nature of the French or the Chinese.

Moreover, the claim that the rest of the wicked characters are Christians, besides overlooking a minor Jewish character, the repulsive Barney (Fagin's associate), simply ignores the extent to which Dickens was willing to draw on the long history of anti-Semitic associations and stereotypes to provide added resonance to Fagin's particular villainies. In addition, Fagin has certain prominent physical characteristics of the stereotyped stage Jew, notably his red hair, which is repeatedly referred to; in Cruikshank's illustrations, Fagin is also shown with hooked nose, broad-brimmed hat, and long gown. Frequently described by Dickens as skulking or creeping stealthily through the back alleys of London, Fagin is frightening and repulsive as well. Furthermore, he is a dealer in second-hand clothes and trinkets, one of the few occupations open to Jews at the time of *Oliver Twist*. However, Dickens does withhold from Fagin other characteristics of the stage-Jew stereotype, for example, the supposedly characteristic gestures and "Jewish" speech patterns such as lisp, dialect, or nasal intonation displayed by other Jews in Dickens's fiction (including Barney in *Oliver Twist*). Fagin's English is as improbably pure as Oliver's.[4]

More fundamental to Fagin's conformity to the popular Jewish stereotype, however, are his clear identification with the devil (shared with Shylock) and his ominous role as an abductor of children and violator of childhood innocence.[5] Both associations have been credited with providing much of the impetus to anti-Semitism from medieval times through our own. Fagin resembles the devil first of all in appearance. The red beard worn by Fagin was worn by the devil in medieval drama, before being transferred to the Jew. Thus, Fagin's red hair signified the union of the devil and the Jew. Moreover, when we – and Oliver – first meet Fagin in his "lair," he is described, devil-like, as standing over the fire, toasting fork in hand, and surrounded by the children who constitute his gang:

In a frying-pan, which was on the fire ... some sausages were cooking; and standing over them, with a toasting fork in his hand, was a very old shrivelled Jew, whose villainous-looking and repulsive face was obscured by a quantity of matted red hair. He was dressed in a greasy flannel gown with his throat bare ... Seated round the table were four or five boys, none older than the Dodger ... These all crowded about their associate as he whispered a few words to the Jew; and then turned round and grinned at Oliver. So did the Jew himself, toasting-fork in hand.[6]

In Cruikshank's illustration, Fagin's "toasting-fork" bears a close family resemblance to a pitch-fork, and in subsequent scenes the fire, with Fagin either toasting something over it, brooding over it, or fanning it with a bellows, is an inevitable presence in "the Jew's" "den" or "lair."

In addition to repeating the associations between Fagin and the fire that can be seen as a stand-in for more engulfing Hell Fires, Dickens also refers to Fagin in a number of places as "the merry old gentleman," a description that denoted the devil. Fagin is even identified as the devil by various characters who have reason to know him well. For example, when Fagin enters the room of the criminal, Bill Sikes, Sikes rebukes his growling dog, "Lie down, you stupid brute! Don't you know the devil when he's got a great coat on?" (187), an association which Sikes suggests again later on:

"I don't feel like myself when you lay that withered old claw on my shoulder, so take it away", said Sikes casting off the Jew's hand.

"It makes you nervous, Bill – reminds you of being nabbed, does it?" said Fagin ...

"Reminds me of being nabbed by the devil," returned Sikes. "There never was another man with such a face as yours, unless it was your father, and I suppose *he* is singeing his grizzled red beard by this time, unless you came straight from the old 'un without any father at all betwixt you." (398)

In a scene partly reminiscent of this, as well as of the instinctive aversion felt by all virtuous characters toward the devil in medieval folklore, the good-hearted prostitute Nancy "shrank back, as Fagin offered to lay his hand on hers" (401). Later, recalling Fagin's role in having "led her, step by step, deeper and deeper down into an abyss of crime and misery, whence was no escape" (397), Nancy refers to Fagin as "Devil that he is, and worse than devil as he has been to me" (412).

The image of Fagin as devil is further reinforced by his function in the novel, which is to entice Oliver into abandoning the ways of righteousness and participating in evil. Fagin is in cahoots with Oliver's half-brother, Monks. By the provisions of their father's will, Oliver will lose his share of their mutual inheritance if he departs from the path of virtue. Seeking to corrupt Oliver, Fagin is playing for no less a stake than the boy's immortal soul. Fagin's aim is to win Oliver over through the boy's own deliberate choice. To this end Fagin first keeps Oliver in lonely isolation and then offers him, as an alternative, the fellowship of his gang of young thieves. At first the program seems to be succeeding: "the wily old Jew had the boy in his toils. Having prepared his mind, by solitude and gloom, to prefer any society to the companionship of his own sad thoughts in such a dreary place, he was now slowly instilling into his soul the poison which he hoped would blacken it, and change its hue for ever" (185). Shortly thereafter, plotting a robbery in which Oliver is to be an indispensible tool, Fagin says triumphantly, "Once let him feel that he is one of us; once fill his mind with the idea that he has been a thief; and he's ours! Ours for his life." To which Sikes objects,

"Ours! ... Yours, you mean."
"Perhaps I do, my dear," said the Jew with a shrill chuckle. "Mine, if you like, Bill." (192)

In seeking to instill into Oliver's "soul the poison which he hoped would blacken it and change its hue for ever," Fagin is conforming to another of the reiterated medieval stereotypes of the Jew, the Jew as poisoner (of Christians, of wells), an image which, of course, has been exploited with terrible consequences in our own times. In fact, before inciting Sikes to the murder of

Nancy, Fagin makes a concerted effort to persuade Nancy to poison Sikes, assuring her, "I have the means at hand, quiet and close" (401).

A figure of primordial and ubiquitous evil, Fagin conveys a sense of overpowering and almost supernatural horror that gains force from his being frequently seen through the eyes of defenceless childhood innocence, against which he is perpetually conspiring. At times he is lacking even the "humanoid" characteristics of the more familiar devil figure. For example:

The mud lay thick upon the stones, and a black mist hung over the streets; the rain fell sluggishly down, and everything felt cold and clammy to the touch. It seemed just the night when it befitted such a being as the Jew to be abroad. As he glided stealthily along, creeping beneath the shelter of the walls and doorways, the hideous old man seemed like some loathsome reptile, engendered in the slime and darkness through which he moved: crawling forth by night, in search of some rich offal for a meal. (186)

Or again, near the end:

Fagin sat watching in his old lair, with face so distorted and pale, and eyes so red and bloodshot, that he looked less like a man, than like some hideous phantom, moist from the grave, and worried by an evil spirit ... His right hand was raised to his lips, and as, absorbed in thought, he bit his long black nails, he disclosed among his toothless gums a few such fangs as should have been a dog's or rat's.

In his cell the night before his execution, while we are reminded that "His red hair hung down upon his bloodless face" (470), we are also told that his "countenance [was] more like that of a snared beast than the face of a man" (472).

The image of the Jew as dog had, of course, appeared in Shakespeare. The image of the Jew as loathsome reptile, crawling forth by night in search of some rich offal for a meal, conjures up the spectre of Jew as devourer of innocent flesh and/or blood, engaged in unholy ceremonies of a mysterious, monstrous, primitive nature. Indeed, as I have suggested, Fagin's very status as the enticer and kidnapper of children, whom he then seeks to use in his own evil pursuits, carries with it echoes of William of Norwich, Hugh of Lincoln and the whole familiar complex of charges against the Jew (discussed in Allen Koretsky's essay on Chaucer), ranging from abduction of Christian children, to their ritual (or brute) murder and mutilation, to profane feasts.[7]

At once "demoniacal" (189) and subhuman, (both these aspects of the Jew existed in late medieval and Renaissance literature, as Derek Cohen's and Ross Arthur's chapters show), Fagin is nonetheless more potentially menacing to Oliver than he is in fact, and than he has been to others. Fagin's potential for bloodshed is suggested on Oliver's second view of him. Thinking the boy to be asleep, Fagin draws from its hiding place a box of jewels which he proceeds to admire, while congratulating himself on the expeditious execution of former gang members: "What a fine thing capital punishment is! Dead men never repent; dead men never bring awkward stories to light. Ah, it's a fine thing for the trade! Five of 'em strung up in a row" (107). Oliver, however, is not asleep, but rather in "a drowsy state, between sleeping and waking" (106). When Fagin sees himself observed, "He closed the lid of the box with a loud crash; and, laying his hand on a bread knife which was on the table, started furiously up. He trembled very much though; for, even in his terror Oliver could see that the knife quivered in the air" (108). The quivering knife, echoing the blood libel accusation of centuries, remains emblematically poised in the reader's – and doubtless Oliver's – imagination, though it is in fact never used.

In a similar state between sleep and waking (a phenomenon Dickens is at some pains to describe and which casts a somewhat surreal aura over the scene),[8] Oliver has another terrifying vision of Fagin later in the novel, after Oliver has been rescued a second time from "the Jew's" clutches and is recuperating in the idyllic pastoral residence of the Maylies. Fagin and Oliver's evil half-brother, Monks, track him down there, and, as if emerging from Oliver's sleeping consciousness, suddenly appear before the boy's eyes, outside his window. But by the time Oliver has roused himself to call for help, his enemies have disappeared without a trace; his protectors search for footprints or other evidence but are unable to find anything, which suggests that Fagin and Monks have somehow disappeared from the scene by supernatural means (309–12).

This supernatural note is sounded only once; the insistence on Fagin's unremitting evil, however, is pervasive. The evil that Fagin represents is, indeed, so inclusive – one might even say, so generic – that although we are treated to a highly dramatic trial scene in the penultimate chapter, no specific *charge* against Fagin is ever mentioned. The omission is significant. It suggests that something as finite as an explicit charge could only mitigate or trivialize the enormity of the villain's all-encompassing evil. The scene is, incidentally, strikingly different from Dickens's other famous trial scene, in *Great Expectations*, written some two dozen years later, in which the transported criminal, Magwitch, though also guilty of more serious sins, is explicitly condemned to death for having defied the terms of his earlier sentence by having returned to England. Dickens's account of Magwitch's trial is also memorable for its compassion with the accused and its distaste for the titillated onlookers. Not so with Fagin, who reads his only too-well-deserved verdict in the faces of the spectators:

Looking round, he saw that the jurymen had turned together, to consider of their verdict. As his eyes wandered to the gallery, he could see the people rising above each other to see his face: some hastily applying their glasses to their eyes, and others whispering their neighbours with looks expressive of abhorrence. A few there were, who seemed unmindful of him, and looked only to the jury, in impatient wonder how they could delay. But in no one face ... could he read the faintest sympathy with himself, or any feeling but one of all-absorbing interest that he should be condemned. (466)

When the jury returns,

Perfect stillness ensued – not a rustle – not a breath – Guilty.
  The building rang with a tremendous shout, and another, and another, and then it echoed loud groans, then gathered strength as they swelled out, like angry thunder. It was a peal of joy from the populace outside, greeting the news that he would die on Monday. (467–8)

Vox Populi, vox Dei.[9]
  Having declared war on society and humankind, Fagin is justly repudiated by it, while Oliver finds salvation through his steadfast moral rejection of Fagin's band of outlaws and his integration into respectable society and assumption of his rightful position there. Fagin, in fact, as Dickens makes plain, has cut himself off from any specifically Jewish community as well. When we first meet him, it is *sausages* he is roasting over that fire, and later we watch him breakfasting on ham (109). The night before his execution we are shown a glimpse – for the first and only time – of a different kind of Jew: "Venerable men of his own persuasion had come to pray beside him, but he had driven them away with curses. They renewed their charitable efforts, and he beat them off" (469). The fact that Fagin is a bad Jew, a voluntary outsider to the Jewish community, does not

detract from the fact that his badness throughout the novel is presented as inextricable from his identity as "the Jew." Fagin's villainy, as we have seen, gains resonance and added horror from Dickens's insistence on Fagin's Jewishness and Dickens's readiness to exploit the whole compendium of terrifying associations that have clustered around the stereotype of the Jew in the popular imagination from the Middle Ages onward: the Jew as devil (or his close associate), as subhuman monster, as poisoner, as kidnapper, mutilator, murderer of innocent Christian children, on whom, perhaps, he cannibalistically feeds in observance of alien rituals. This is not to suggest − nor has it ever seriously been suggested − that Dickens was attempting to incite anti-Semitic feeling or to fan the fires of anti-Semitism. Rather, Dickens seems to have been appealing to an anti-Semitism already present in his readers, which he was simply willing to exploit in creating his first major representation of evil in its confrontation with childhood innocence. Of course, taken as a whole, Dickens's novels present a wide array of evil characters, only one of whom is a Jew. But it must be acknowledged that in his portrayal of Fagin's villainy, Dickens, as a young writer, chose to rely on ready-made, deeply rooted associations to a supposedly specifically Jewish brand of villainy.

I n a study of the revisions of *Oliver Twist* Dickens did for an edition in 1867, Lauriat Lane, Jr, has shown that, in the chapter showing Fagin awaiting his execution, "Dickens replaced the epithet ['the Jew'] at every possible point by the name 'Fagin,' thereby emphasizing the real individual rather than the archetypal racial villain." Lane further asserts, "By dwelling so fully on 'Fagin's Last Night Alive,' and by later revising this chapter as he did, Dickens set up a bond of sympathy between us and the villain ... By this sympathy, Fagin's character is changed from what it is elsewhere in the novel." It is certainly interesting to know that Dickens made these changes, and Lane may be right that the revisions showed Dickens was "determined to atone even further" (than he had through the creation of Riah) and that they "arose out of a genuine feeling of guilt."[10] However, I cannot agree that Dickens's revisions have the effect of setting up a genuine "bond of sympathy between us and the villain," whatever the author's conscious intentions may have been. Quite the contrary. Fagin had to be humanized in order to gratify the reader's need to see Fagin get the punishment he so amply deserved – to see him suffer real *Todesangst* and be genuinely hanged. The point to be made in the context of this study, however, is that Dickens could not un-Jewify Fagin, even if he wanted to. A Fagin who was not "the Jew" would, quite simply, not be the nightmare villain whom Dickens created in *Oliver Twist*.

How are we to understand the transition from the diabolical Fagin to the patriarchal Mr Riah? One explanation, offered by Edmund Wilson, is simply the duality of Dickens's imagination. In Dickens's prodigious output, Wilson points out, we can find a bad and a good exemplum of many types: in different novels he creates a bad manufacturer and a good manufacturer, a bad dwarf and a good dwarf, a bad and rebellious illegitimate daughter and a good and submissive illegitimate daughter, etc. Hence Dickens had to balance the bad Jew, Fagin, with the good Jew, Mr Riah.[11] Another, and not contradictory, explanation that has been suggested is the liberalizing attitudes of the Victorian temper, which made Dickens responsive to Mrs Davis' observations. Between 1830 and 1860 there was "a steady rise in the status of English Jewry. Legal barriers were swept away, commercial restrictions removed, and social antagonisms lessened." In 1830 there were twenty to thirty thousand Jews in England, most of whom were peddlers, traders in old clothes, or money-lenders. "A Jew could not open a shop ... [in] London, be called to the Bar, receive a university degree, or sit in Parliament."[12] During the next thirty years the situation changed radically; in 1858 Baron Lionel Rothschild had taken a seat in Parliament and England was on its way to having a Jewish Prime Minister, albeit a converted one.

Dickens's own attitudes may well have reflected the liberalizing trends of the times. As a young man and editor of *Bentley's Miscellany*, Dickens had published some very anti-Semitic sketches, and in his letters of the 1830s and 1840s he uses the term "Jew" as one of abuse, denoting unscrupulous financial dealings (even when the perpetrator is not Jewish).[13] By the 1850s, though Dickens continued to publish articles with traces of anti-Semitism in his own periodicals, *Household Words* and *All the Year Round*, the anti-Semitism was much milder than what had appeared earlier in *Bentley's Miscellany*. And in 1851, in his *Child's History of England*, he did speak out against the persecution of the Jews, as he was later to remind Mrs Davis.

Yet Dickens's personal attitude to the Jews remained less than heartening from a modern perspective. In 1860, preparing the sale of his London residence, Tavistock House, to the Davises, he wrote, "If the Jew Money-Lender buys (I say 'if,' because of course I shall never believe him until he has paid the money)." When the sale went through he wrote: "Tavistock House is cleared to-day, and possession delivered up to the new tenant. I must say that in all things the purchaser has behaved thoroughly well, and that I cannot call to mind any occasion when I have had money-dealings with anyone that have been so satisfactory, considerate and trusting."[14] It was, of course the wife of the "Jew Money-Lender" whose correspondence with Dickens provided the impetus for his creation of Mr Riah.

M r Riah is conceived in many ways as a stark contrast (and hence, corrective) to Fagin, though he is by no means central to *Our Mutual Friend*, as Fagin is to *Oliver Twist*. Riah personifies honesty (in financial dealings, in human relations), loyalty, integrity, humility, and disinterested benevolent concern for the unfortunate and the vulnerable. An Old Testament patriarch (though singularly devoid of any righteous indignation or rage), in his interview with his employer he first appears to the reader as "an old Jewish man in an ancient coat, long of skirt, and wide of pocket. A venerable man, bald and shining at the top of his head, and with long grey hair flowing down at its sides and mingling with his beard. A man who with a graceful Eastern action of homage bent his head, and stretched out his hands with the palms downward, as if to deprecate the wrath of a superior."[15] Of his clothing, we read, "In the entry hung his rusty large-brimmed low-crowned hat, as long out of date as his coat; in the corner near it stood his staff – no walking-stick but a veritable staff" (328). Of his ascent up the staircase, "As he toiled on before, with his palm upon the stair-rail, and his long black skirt, a very gaberdine, overhanging each successive step, he might have been the leader in some pilgrimage of devotional ascent to a prophet's tomb" (332).

Perhaps the most striking contrast between Fagin and Riah, however, lies in their relations to children and young adults. Where Fagin was the menacing exploiter of childhood innocence (who posed as convivial gang leader), Riah is a – more sober – benevolent protector. Riah offers shelter, moral support and "book-learning" to two industrious and virtuous young women (probably teenagers) whom he has taken under his wing: the humpbacked Jenny Wren, daughter of an abusive alcoholic father, and Lizzie Hexam, orphaned daughter of a "riverman" who made his living fishing corpses out of the Thames.

Jenny's term of endearment for Mr Riah is "fairy godmother" or "godmother" for short, suggesting not only his role as benefactor and protector but also his somewhat androgynous status. As we see him "stealing through the streets in his ancient dress, like the ghost of a departed Time" (465), the "long black skirt" is mentioned time and again: his "long-skirted coat" (462); "his grave and measured pace, staff in hand, skirt at heel" (480); and when Jenny learns of her father's death, she seeks comfort from her fairy godmother by "hiding her face in the Jewish skirts" (801). Might it be that the special mythical dimension claimed for this "venerable", "ancient" figure can best be established if he is seen as, somehow, beyond anything so commonplace as a clear-cut sexual identity?

Certainly he is lightyears away from any personal sexual self-interest, a fact indispensible to his role as protector of both Jenny and Lizzie, and particularly crucial in his relation to Lizzie, whose "virtue" and "innocence" are threatened in a more specifically Victorian way than Oliver's. She is in love with the well-born lawyer, Eugene Wrayburn, who is strongly attracted to her and esteems her, but hardly contemplates making her his wife. Made aware of the danger ("he was not of her station ... Perils were closing round her, and the circle was fast darkening" [490]), Riah assists Lizzie in her desire to flee temptation by arranging for her employment by fellow Jews who own a paper-mill some distance from London. (Of her employers Lizzie will subsequently relate, "The gentleman certainly is a Jew ... and the lady, his wife, is a Jewess, and I was first brought to their notice by a Jew. But I think there cannot be kinder people in the world" [579]. That "but" may not please us, but it certainly is candid: the frank admission of prior expectations happily confuted.) In his generous, selfless concern for Lizzie's welfare, Riah contrasts sharply with Fagin, who corrupts Nancy for his own gain. However, it should be observed that Fagin's mythic status, like Riah's, also precludes anything so banal as sexual self-interest.[16] In his role as Victorian defender of maiden virtue, Riah in fact resembles an earlier Dickens figure, the avuncular (and hence, sexless) Mr Pickwick, though Riah has none of Pickwick's fun-loving high spirits.

Riah does, however, have a most unfortunate job. He is the "front" or, as Mrs Lammle puts it, the "mask" (688) for the unscrupulous money lender, Fascination Fledgeby, who conceals

his own boundless avarice and viciousness behind the imper-
sonal-sounding institution of Pubsey and Co. Forced to transmit
to Pubsey's clients the ruthless terms insisted on by his employer, Riah is invariably misperceived as the author of those
terms, despite his repeated assertions that he is not the principal of the company but merely the servant of another. This
comedy of errors is a source of endless perverse delight to Fledgeby, who loses no opportunity to vilify Riah before others ("He
is a thorough Jew to look at, but he is a more thorough Jew to
deal with" [634–5], Fledgeby assures one client) and to insult
him openly to his face, as Fledgeby untiringly sustains for his
own private amusement the masquerade he himself has constructed: "'Now, old 'un!' cried Fascination, in his light raillery,
'what dodgery are you up to next, sitting there with your eyes
shut? You ain't asleep. Catch a weasel at it, and catch a Jew!'"
(481). In the face of Fledgeby's unceasing anti-Semitic taunts,
Riah can only question meekly, "Do you not, sir – without in-
tending it ... sometimes mingle the character I fairly earn in
your employment, with the character which it is your policy that
I should bear?" (482).

That the epitome of integrity and benevolence should find
himself in such a situation is humanly implausible, a problem
of which Dickens was obviously aware when he provided a human explanation in terms of both Riah's poverty and his loyalty:
"'I had sickness and misfortunes, and was so poor,' said the old
man, 'as hopelessly to owe the father, principal and interest.
The son inheriting, was so merciful as to forgive me both, and
place me here'" (329). And Dickens underlines the point by
further referring to Riah as Fledgeby's "grateful servant – in
whose race gratitude is deep, strong, and enduring" (335). However, the symbolic significance of Riah's role is obviously more
important to Dickens than the role's plausibility. Historically,
as is well known, because of the medieval church's prohibition
against "usury," Jews had been not merely permitted but encouraged to become moneylenders so that they might provide
the Christian ruling-classes of the countries in which they lived
with a ready source of liquid capital. At the same time, this
made them convenient scapegoats in times of difficulty.[17] Often
barred from owning land and from respectable occupations,
Jews were, in other words, engineered into a situation in which
they were targets for abuse and persecution. The conception of
Riah, then, and his relation to Fledgeby, is informed by the
wider social-historical perspective that is characteristic of

Dickens's later novels, a perspective Dickens makes explicit in a scene in which Riah knocks on Fledgeby's "door with the top of his staff, and, having listened, sat down on the threshold. It was characteristic of his habitual submission, that he sat down on the raw dark staircase, as many of his ancestors had probably sat down in dungeons, taking what befell him as it might befall" (480).

Gleefully casting Riah in the role of merciless Shylock in front of Jenny Wren, however, Fascination Fledgeby finally overplays his hand. His gratification in having Jenny turn on Riah ("You are not the godmother at all! ... You are ... the wicked Wolf!" [638]) is temporary. Jenny's disillusion with Riah provides the – implausibly belated – stimulus for Riah to become "hateful to myself" and to reject his employment by Fledgeby, reflecting – again belatedly and again with more symbolic than human credibility – on the special collective responsibility of the Jews:

I reflected ... that I was doing dishonour to my ancient faith and race. I reflected ... that in bending my neck to the yoke I was willing to wear, I bent the unwilling necks of the whole Jewish people. For it is not, in Christian countries, with the Jews as with other peoples. Men say, "This is a bad Greek, but there are good Greeks. This is a bad Turk, but there are good Turks." Not so with the Jews ... they take the worst of us as samples of the best ... and they say "All Jews are alike." If, doing what I was content to do here, because I was grateful for the past ... I had been a Christian, I could have done it, compromising no one but my individual self. But doing it as a Jew, I could not choose but compromise the Jews of all conditions and all countries. It is a little hard upon us, but it is the truth. I would that all our people remembered it! (795)

Here, as everywhere in the novel, Riah emerges as more symbol than human being. It should hardly be necessary to reiterate the frequently made observation that, as a dramatic character, Riah totally lacks Fagin's exuberant vitality. As one critic, writing of the unrealistic tradition of the "good Jew" to which Riah belongs, aptly puts it, "Riah and his type will not bleed if you prick them."[18]

Moving from *Oliver Twist* to *Our Mutual Friend*, then, as the Jew has been transformed from exploiter to protector of innocent children, he has also moved from victimizer to victim, Riah being identified through his own victimization with the victimized young women he seeks to protect. However, this leads us to observe a striking similarity between Dickens's two Jewish characters, for all their many differences. Both are outcasts from the dominant society. Fagin, as mythic incarnation of evil, has cut himself off from kinship with the human community; but Riah, though part of a "networking" *Jewish* community, is also estranged from the broader society in which he lives. This comes about in part through his own noble, mythic quality, in part through that society's anti-Semitism, but perhaps in greatest part through his chosen identification with society's other victims and outcasts such as Jenny Wren and Lizzie Hexam.

In presenting his earlier Jewish character, Dickens scarcely distinguished between outcast and outlaw; Fagin was both, and this was a measure of his evil. Riah, on the other hand, is an outcast but by no means an outlaw. Indeed, he and the other marginal figures, such as Jenny, Lizzie, and the all-but-impoverished Betty Higden (fleeing institutionalized charity with her burial money sewn into her clothing), are as central to the moral consciousness of the novel, and the establishment of its moral norms, as are the good characters who form the nucleus of the John Harmon plot (that is, Harmon/Rokesmith and the Boffins). Dickens's different perspectives on outcasts reflect an important shift between the writing of the two novels in his view of society itself, a shift that is more certain and more profound than any presumed change in his view of Jews, in whom he never seems to have been greatly interested. In *Oliver Twist*, despite a bitter satiric attack on specific social institutions such as the work house and the New Poor Law, as well as on corrupt, self-seeking representatives of respectable society such as Mr Bumble (a beadle), it remains true that society, which ultimately tries and condemns Fagin, for all its flaws represents the moral norm. In *Our Mutual Friend*, however, it is Society itself – here spelled with a capital "S" – that is put on trial, and, though not without ambiguities, found clearly wanting.

Indeed, in *Our Mutual Friend*, Good Society is shown to be almost indistinguishable from the criminal element which it sustains and abets. Fascination Fledgeby, for example, is a distant relative of Twemlow, who is the sole (though feeble) positive representative of society and a first cousin to the much mentioned Lord Snigsworth. But Fledgeby is also a friend and accomplice of the criminal Lammles, who are taken up and fêted by society until their public bankruptcy forces them to go abroad. Fledgeby, in fact, is described as "a kind of outlaw in the bill-broking line ... His circle of familiar acquaintances, from

Mr. Lammle round, all had a touch of the outlaw, as to their rovings in the merry greenwood of Jobbery Forest, lying on the outskirts of the Share-Market and the Stock Exchange" (324). Moreover, it is Fledgeby himself, posing as Riah's benefactor (he is addressed by Riah as "Generous Christian master" [328]) and in reality his tormentor, who is cast in the "traditional" Shylock role. This noxious loanshark, in addition, takes on some of the attributes of Dickens's earlier Jewish villain. Alfred Lammle, who knows Fledgeby well, assures his wife, "When money is in question with that young fellow, he is a match for the Devil" (319). And in the scene in which Fledgeby forces Riah to act the Shylock before the well-meaning Twemlow and Jenny Wren, Fledgeby is twice described by Fagin's (and the devil's) adjective, "merry." In fact, in Fledgeby's malice toward Riah we may recognize something of the "diabolical" malice of the classic anti-Semite: it has no discernible cause, other than Fledgeby's own nagging feelings of inferiority (he is forever fingering his chin in the hope of detecting the first sproutings of a beard) and his inborn viciousness.

More is involved in Fledgeby's designation as an outlaw than Dickens's almost medieval repugnance for some of the basic institutions of capitalism – as powerful an element in his work as this always is. Though "a kind of outlaw" and possibly a diabolical one at that, Fledgeby is not isolated and detachable from the social fabric as Fagin had been. Rather, Fledgeby is part and parcel of a society that is characterized in its very essence by the corrupt and corrupting pursuit of wealth and the worship of false social values and status. If Fledgeby finds a "back-up" in the Lammles, they, in turn, are the protegés of the "brannew" (48) Mr and Mrs Veneering, who are also destined to end in insolvency abroad, but not before Mr Veneering has risen to the august rank of Member of Parliament, having paved his way by giving innumerable dinner parties at which he hosts: the unforgettable Podsnap, exemplary specimen of mindless, patriotic British self-satisfaction and arrogance; the empty, artifically (and not very well) preserved, self-dramatizing Lady Tippins; the decent but befuddled Twemlow (first cousin to Lord Snigsworth); and many other representatives of a stupid, proud, self-righteous, self-serving and heartless (but respectable) Society.[19] At the lower echelons of this society, obsessed with maintaining his hard-won respectability and also with another, even more destructive passion, is Lizzie's would-be suitor, the schoolmaster Bradley Headstone, a murderer at heart and, finally, a murderer in deed.

When all this is said, however, one habitual guest at the Veneerings' dinners for Society does pose a special problem for our understanding of Riah's place in the novel. It is a problem that has simply been ignored by critics who have written about Dickens's "good Jew."

Eugene Wrayburn, Lizzie's idle, aimless seducer manqué, will, by the end of the novel, undergo a near death by drowning (at the hands of Bradley Headstone), be fished out of the river by Lizzie and, expecting not to live, marry her as a kind of reparation for his dishonourable intentions toward her and her noble love for him. As a sexual threat to a virtuous maiden of inferior class, Eugene is punished at least as harshly as *Jane Eyre's* Mr Rochester; so severely maimed is Eugene by Headstone's murderous assault that, the day after the marriage, Dickens refers to "the utter helplessness of the wreck of him" (824). However, by the end of the novel, like Mr Rochester, Eugene is on the road to physical and moral recovery and is prepared to embark upon a new life of domestic virtue and vocational diligence. The near-villain is, in short, chastised, reformed, and, in the end, placed alongside Harmon/Rokesmith as one of the novel's heroes.

In addition to his idleness and sexual arrogance, Eugene is guilty of another offence, one that is never punished or even adequately acknowledged: his insulting, anti-Semitic remarks to Riah in front of Lizzie. In a disturbing scene, Riah comes upon Lizzie after she has rejected a violent marriage proposal from Bradley Headstone and has, in consequence, been brutally cast off by her brother, one of Headstone's pupils. Extending words of comfort, Riah is preparing to take Lizzie to his home to recover her composure, when they are intercepted by Eugene, who ignores Lizzie's request that he leave her alone with Riah. "'But, Lizzie, I came expressly to join you. I came to walk home with you ... And I have been lingering about,' added Eugene, 'like a bailiff; or,' with a look at Riah, 'an old clothesman'" (463).

Despite Lizzie's identification of Riah as her "protector" and "a trustworthy friend," Eugene proceeds,

"If Mr. Aaron," said Eugene, who soon found this fatiguing, will be good enough to relinquish his charge to me, he will be quite free for any engagement he may have at the Synagogue. Mr. Aaron, will you have the kindness?"

But the old man stood stock still.

"Good evening, Mr. Aaron," said Eugene, politely; "we need not detain you." Then turning to Lizzie, "Is our friend Mr. Aaron a little deaf?" (464)

Like Fledgeby, who in one scene refers to Riah repeatedly as "Judah" (786), Eugene uses the name of a venerable Hebrew forefather to deprive Riah of his human individuality and replace it with a collective racial designation, a standard anti-Semitic ploy. The anti-Semitism implicit in Eugene's suggestion that Riah would prefer to be "free for any engagement he may have at the Synagogue" to escorting a Christian maiden to safety scarcely needs underlining. For the rest of the scene Eugene continues to refer to Mr Riah as Mr Aaron. Riah remains with Lizzie at her request, but she is not strong enough to insist on Eugene's leaving them. Together, Eugene and Riah escort her to her home, "Nothing more being said of repairing to Riah's" (465).

So gross and offensive is Eugene's treatment of Riah in this scene that we might expect his moral reformation at the end to include some self-reproach or repentance for this ugly aspect of his conduct. But there is none. And after Lizzie's departure from London, thanks to Riah's assistance, she is never shown with Riah again. He is not even invited to her wedding, which would be the traditional occasion for reconciliation and forgiveness, in literature as in life. The reformed Eugene is made to seek forgiveness only from Lizzie; his abuse to her "protector" and "trustworthy friend" is somehow forgotten, swept under the carpet.

Perhaps we are to understand that Eugene acknowledges and repents of his glib anti-Semitism along with his other "gentlemanly" vices, but the tradition within which Dickens is working would seem to call for something more explicit. Fascination Fledgeby, when exposed as the true power behind Pubsey and Co., has his mouth crammed with salt and snuff by Alfred Lammle, who then administers "as furious and sound a thrashing as even Mr. Fledgeby merited" (792). Jenny Wren, who has suffered bitterly from Fledgeby's misrepresentation of Riah, vindicates her fairy godmother, whom she had been led temporarily to renounce, by sticking pepper, vinegar, and brown paper on all of Fledgeby's open wounds. Both Riah's abusers meet their come-uppance, but in Eugene's case, unlike Fledgeby's, this is not specifically related to his abuse of Riah.

While this may leave us with a sense of something unresolved with regard to Riah's place in the novel, the issue of anti-Semitism was obviously not foremost in Dickens's mind when he wrote *Our Mutual Friend*. Riah is, after all, only an important minor character, not a major one, and any explicit correction of Eugene's anti-Semitism might have detoured Dickens in directions he did not wish to pursue. And if Riah is not brought together with Lizzie after her departure from London or her subsequent marriage, he does not altogether disappear; the opportune death of Jenny's alcoholic father opens the way for Riah to move in with the orphaned girl. In Jenny's last appearance, she explains to a visitor, underscoring again Riah's androgynous and mythic status, "[I] live here with my fairy godmother ... With my second father. Or with my first, for that matter" (881).

For the virtuous orphaned children, the Happy Ending in *Our Mutual Friend*, as in *Oliver Twist*, is still their integration into the larger social fabric; but in the later novel this integration is more tentative, and the happiness it is destined to bring is more open to question. We see Jenny about, perhaps, to embark on a romance with the youthful and unglamorous Sloppy, the late Betty Higden's charge, who has recently been adopted by the newly wealthy Boffins. Lizzie, through her marriage to Eugene, is indeed on the road to integration into Society, but we cannot forget that this same Society has been the consistent object of the novelist's biting satire, while the outcast status of the virtuous Riah and his victimized protegées has served as an implicit moral critique of the society from which they are excluded. Oliver Twist's "fairy godfather," Mr Brownlow, on the other hand, had stood for goodness and social respectability at the same time, a combination achieved in *Our Mutual Friend* by only a few characters, such as the ineffectual Twemlow or the notoriously unsatisfactory hero, Harmon/Rokesmith. In the last chapter of *Our Mutual Friend*, Twemlow speaks with what is apparently intended as the most intelligent possible "Voice of Society": "If this gentleman's feelings of gratitude, of respect, of admiration, and affection, induced him ... to marry this lady, I think he is the greater gentleman for the action and makes her the greater lady. I beg to say, that when I use the word, gentleman, I use it in the sense in which the degree may be attained by any man" (891). But the Veneerings' guests regard his remarks with skepticism from one perspective, and we readers may harbour doubts of an opposite kind, wondering whether Eugene is indeed a gentleman "in the sense in which the degree may be attained by any man," and whether marrying him and entering Society is the reward Lizzie's noble nature deserves.

By looking at Dickens's two most important Jewish characters, we can chart some of the fundamental changes in his moral and social outlook in the quarter century or so that separates *Oliver Twist* from *Our Mutual Friend*. Both Jews are outcasts from the dominant society. But the position of outcast, which was a mark of the Jew's evil in the earlier book, becomes a badge of his righteousness in the later one, as the outcast has moved from villainous victimizer to virtuous victim. Society, which conferred salvation on Oliver and righteously tried and condemned Fagin in *Oliver Twist*, is itself on trial in *Our Mutual Friend*, and is shown to have greater power to corrupt than to save. Evil is no longer isolated in individuals, however mythic, who may be seen as being at war with society; rather, evil is inextricably woven into the social fabric itself. If Dickens's portrait of Fagin is unremittingly black, his ultimate vision of human possibility in *Oliver Twist* is (though somewhat unconvincingly) bright, whereas his idealized portrait of Mr Riah only serves to intensify the darkness that hovers over the world of *Our Mutual Friend*, despite Dickens's inconclusive gestures toward a happy ending.

CHAPTER FOUR

Constructing the Contradiction: Anthony Trollope's The Way We Live Now

DEREK COHEN

Trollope's construction of Jewish identity in *The Way We Live Now* (1875) is complicated by the fact that not only its Jews but almost all of the novel's characters are presented negatively: that is, the very catholicity of the author's rage against the society implied in his title tempts some readers into the belief that the Jewish crimes and cupidities are merely another species of corruption in a frantically declining moral world. Indeed, such a reading is justified to some extent by the fact that it is a Jew, Ezekiel Breghert, who performs one of the few honourable – if passionless – acts of love in the novel. That is, Jews are allowed to possess virtues as well as vices, much like the Christians of the book. It is, however, the symbolic connotations which Trollope attaches to his Jews that give the lie to this liberal reading of the text, a reading which is determinedly tolerant of and apologetic for the many shifts of direction towards stereotyping and racial hatred. The central figure of the novel, Augustus Melmotte, a Jewish financier, is much more than a crook; he is an object of fear and the possessor of enormous power that he has garnered by his cynical manipulation of the greed and dishonesty rampant amongst the English middle class and aristocracy.

Melmotte arrives in London after successful but dangerous swindles in Vienna and Paris, where he seems to have amassed enough money to establish himself as one of the wealthiest men in England. He is capable therefore of gathering about himself a mob of money-hungry English aristocrats by the promise – born of superstition – of being able to enrich them through his magic touch. They believe that he can make money breed.

That Melmotte is a Jew is one of his essential qualities. This fact is a matter of both literary convenience and symbolic importance. In constructing his idea of the Jew, Trollope draws on and contributes to prevailing social ideologies, some of which are revealed in other novels he wrote where Jews play roles of such significance that one is hard put not to see Trollope as obsessed by an idea of the menacing presence of this stranger. (It is significant that between 1800 and 1900 England's Jewish population had increased from 8000 to 250,000.) Two complementary notions of the Jew contribute to Trollope's portraits of Melmotte and the novel's other Jews. One is the plethora of stereotypical notions about the physical attributes of Jews that set them apart from the mainstream and make them identifiable to a discerning eye. There is the idea of the Jew as physically repulsive, the "dirty, greasy Jew"[1] who has thick, oily, black hair and swarthy, oily skin. This notion, though present in *The Way We Live Now*'s Breghert, has a curious antecedent in Trollope's *The Prime Minister*. In this novel, the Jew, Lopez, is presented as a partial contradiction of the stereotype, depending upon the point of view of the observer: English gentlemen look upon Lopez and see slime, whereas English gentlewomen see in him handsomeness. In his characterization of Lopez, Trollope implies a quality which will be transformed into an emblem for power in the person of Melmotte – a mysterious sexuality which decent Englishmen recognize to be another form of uncleanness, but which decent Englishwomen have no weapons against. Until they see the light, both Emily Wharton and Lady Glencora are seduced by Lopez's indubitably oleaginous charm. This sexual power must not be underestimated: it alludes to some hidden, mysterious strength of the Jew which, simply put, gives him an unfair advantage in the social wars that were Trollope's concern. There is, in this sense, a compound of disgust and superstitious envy in the construction of the Jew's physicality. The thing about strong Jews which, Trollope's novel suggests, ought to repel all right-thinking people, attracts them instead. Indeed, on occasion it seems to attract Trollope, against his better judgment. Lopez, for example, is "the kind of man women like" (*The Prime Minister*, 181) because, the narrative and the speaker make clear, women are not capable of the same clarity of vision as men. Trollope's ideas about Jewish physicality and physiognomy are the basis for some of his most telling moral points in *The Way We Live Now*. His ideas about Jewish sexuality as an evil, secret force point fairly directly to Du Maurier's exemplar, Svengali.

In *Nina Balatka* Trollope tries to provide a sympathetic view of the people he so promiscuously excoriates in his other work. The result, by common critical consent, is unhappy in the extreme. The novel is shot through with a kind of sentimental condescension towards its subject, together with a self-indulgent religious tolerance that can give no comfort to readers. Trollope falls into the same nonsensical postures as did Dickens in his well-meant, but finally insulting, portrait of Riah, the good Jew of *Our Mutual Friend*. And it is, ultimately, to Augustus Melmotte and *The Way We Live Now* that we must turn to discover a more authentically felt and subtly achieved construction of Trollope's ideology and for an understanding of the assumptions brought to bear by both him and his public. The novel reveals the powerful presence of enduring notions of what a Jew is and what the Jew stands for. All characters in all novels are to some extent symbolic projections – they all derive from and refer to stereotypes. These stereotypes are distillations of a vast plethora of ideological – historical, political, social, cultural, and personal – assumptions. The novel, its title, its form, and its variegated philosophical presumptions, is an index to its time and to its author's mind. If we are interested in the locus of an ideologically formed construct of the Jew, the novel contributes powerfully to our analysis, for it develops a notion that is rich in historical precedent and it usually confirms the validity of that notion.

Another ideological notion about what a Jew really is that contributes to the portrait of the Jews in *The Way We Live Now* is the notion that Jews have an almost innate affinity to money. They are at home in the world of money, can bask in its lurid gleam and derive a kind of unequal and disproportionate power from touching it without fear of taint. Like Shylock, Fagin, Riah, and a host of minor characters in eighteenth- and nineteenth-century fiction and drama, here again the Jew is associated with money. Shylock lends it, Fagin steals it, but in this novel, as in the works of Marlowe, Shakespeare, and Dickens, the Jew and money are inseparable. It seems to me that a major difference between the despicable Christians of *The Way We Live Now* and the despicable Jews is the Christian awareness of the fact that money can soil and the Jewish attitude of not caring about the soil it carries. That is, the Jews are willing to get their hands dirty in trying to enrich themselves while the Christians just hang about waiting for money to fall into their laps by compromising nothing more labour-intensive than their principles. Work is a virtue in this novel so long as it involves responsible and actual labour; work manipulating money is a vicious and dishonest form of labour, not fit for decent people. As in the case of sexuality, Trollope seems to reveal a contradiction in his attitude towards this aspect of the Jewish character. For, while he deplores the dirty business of acquiring and manipulating fortunes, he reveals a reluctant admiration for the boldness that enables a man to plunge into a world of paper abstractions in order to create a concrete fortune for himself. There is a recognition in the novel of the intestinal fortitude required for the kind of transaction and labour which involves no immediately evident results: recognition that to stake one's life and career on a prospect is both odious and brave.

But these are not the only informing ideas of Jewishness in *The Way We Live Now*. That novel's greatest difficulty lies in the magnitude of its chief character. There is a kind of despairing admiration for this Jewish villain who possesses an alarming virility capable of commanding deference and respect from others. It is significant that at no time is Melmotte brought up short. Nowhere in England does he encounter a man who is prepared to stand up to him, nor one who can discomfort him. Melmotte's confident arrogance is invulnerable and, even as he begins to decline in the eyes and mouths of others, he continues to hold their fear. The only character in the novel who possesses the fortitude to face Melmotte on his own terms is Roger Carbury, a strong, straightforward adherent of standards, values, and virtues that the novel declares to be, most unfortunately, out of date. But Carbury is carefully kept out of Melmotte's sphere – or, rather, keeps himself out of it deliberately – so that Melmotte's dominance of his world remains unchallenged. Melmotte stands as a representative of the new world reflected in the title, a title which proclaims the novel to be a dirge for the way things were. Melmotte is a prince of the values of commerce, enterprise, and exploitation propelled to the throne of success by nerve, energy, and, above all, the greed and cupidity of others. But, just as we must recognize the presence in his character of nerve and energy, and the absence of these qualities in the effete, jejune Englishmen who hope to ride on his coattails to the Disneyland of easy wealth, we must also recognize Trollope's ambivalent admiration for the sheer power that this wicked character has mastered and that he uses to manipulate others. The power reveals itself most vividly in Melmotte's capacity for self-mastery as his fortunes decline, and it is here that the contradiction becomes most relevant.

The chief component of this character, that which gives him his momentum, is the fear he engenders in others. While it would be incorrect to represent this power as a peculiarly Semitic quality, no reader can ignore the way in which Melmotte follows the tradition of Jewish villainy that is embedded in the accepted canon of English literature. Like Marlowe's Barabas, and Shakespeare's Shylock, Melmotte is a financial mainstay of his society who props up the Christians by a villainous desire to control and harm them. Above all, like his predecessors, he has a secret knowledge by which to control them: his knowledge of international finance is represented as the secret of his power. For possessing this privileged awareness of a mysterious universe, he is perceived by the naive Christians who surround him as a kind of magician. As the financial complexities of the novel unravel, the venial, greedy Christians become increasingly confused by the financial system, and increasingly find themselves in the power of this corrupt Jewish financier who seems to them to comprehend and control the world of money. Also like Shylock and Barabas, Melmotte has a daughter who turns out to be an agent in his destruction; she throws in her lot with a man from the enemy camp and gains control over an essential part of her father's fortune.

However, unlike Barabas and Shylock, Melmotte has a wife. She fulfills a passive but essential function in the novel. First, Madame Melmotte is used by the author to display his racial knowledge: Trollope uses her and, much later in the book, Breghert, to define some physical characteristics of the Jewish people. His description of Madame Melmotte is interesting in its assumptions about the ways in which the reader is expected to share in the knowledge of the definitive facts about Jewish physiognomy. Trollope writes: "She was fat and fair – unlike in colour to our traditional Jewesses; but she had the Jewish nose and the Jewish contraction of the eyes."[2] The insinuating way in which he involves the reader in this kind of collusion tells much about Trollope and the novel. It becomes more marked and meaningful in the description of Melmotte himself whose physical appearance indicates not merely that he is a Jew but points to a quality that remains unspecified, elusive, yet dangerous. Trollope is subtle in his insinuation; a notion about a character, once stated, becomes a part of the make-up of that character. Consider, for example, the way in which the editor, Mr Ferdinand Alf, is saddled with the taint of Jewishness without the charge actually being levelled – a neat way of exonerating the narrator from undue hatemongering. His name, Ferdinand, indicates foreignness; it is the name of the deep-dyed Jewish villain of *The Prime Minister*, Ferdinand Lopez. Introducing Alf, Trollope writes, "he was supposed to have been born a German Jew; and certain ladies said that they could distinguish in his tongue the slightest possible foreign accent" (*The Way We Live Now*, I, 8). Mr Alf, later in the novel the opponent of Melmotte for the parliamentary seat of Westminster, has acquired a position of power in society by his efforts as a rather unscrupulous editor of a leading political/literary magazine, *The Evening Pulpit*. As with all of Trollope's Jews who have escaped inclusion in *Nina Balatka*, a puriently sentimental depiction of Jewish life in nineteenth-century Prague, there is and remains a mystery about his origins that is never resolved. As is evident in the quotation above, Alf's origins, like Melmotte's, are a source of society gossip that, though always nominated society gossip and cleverly supplied with the shaky credibility of gossip, is never contradicted. Thus gossip remains the only source of information, and in the absence of a corrective – clearly within the novelist's power – gossip is slowly transmogrified into fact.

One vice to which Jewish men are never subject in Trollope – and, I think, in English literature as a whole – is stupidity. Indeed, the contrary proposition is true of them. Their vice is, often as not, their indisputable cleverness – the very thing about them in other words that destroys them and makes possible a plethora of happy endings in literature. Jewish cleverness is unlike Christian cleverness in that it has no moral base whatever. This lack is both Jewish strength and Jewish weakness: it enables Jews to gain power by a combination of intellectual force and a ruthless willingness to use that force in the interests of achieving power; it is weak in that, in Trollope at least, when it comes into conflict with intelligent upstanding Christianity, it reveals itself as base and hollow. Jews in English literature may be murderers, vicious wife and child beaters, sycophants, manipulators, but they are never fools.

And, unremarkably, these characteristics reveal themselves physiognomically. Augustus Melmotte is described as "a large man, with bushy whiskers and rough thick hair, with heavy eyebrows, and a wonderful look of power about his mouth and chin. This was so strong as to redeem his face from vulgarity; but the countenance and appearances of the man were on the whole unpleasant, and, I may say, untrustworthy" (I, 31). Coming from a tradition of literature which has enjoined readers, not always with subtlety, to refrain from judging from appearances, this puts the author or narrator into a somewhat ambiguous light. This description of Melmotte, while not overtly anti-Semitic, inserts, by the use of clever negation, a series of moral judgments on him and the other Jewish characters of the novel. Though, for example, Melmotte's face is redeemed from vulgarity by power, vulgarity is indisputably present once it has been given form by the mention of its absence. Trollope himself is not so credulous of his narrator that he does not allow himself a small but significant contradiction of this early description in the novel. He later notes of Melmotte that, "It has been already said that Mr. Melmotte was a big man with large whiskers, rough hair, and with an expression of mental power on a harsh vulgar face" (I, 81). So much for the redemption from vulgarity by power quoted above. Vulgarity is given precise articulation later, in the description of Ezekiel Breghert. (This character is the darling of critics who seem to want Trollope to have been less anti-Semitic than the evidence suggests.) Breghert is a rich, Jewish, London financier, a widower of fifty who aspires to the hand of the high-born Miss Longstaffe, whose stupid old father is one of Melmotte's hangers-on. In Breghert's favour it is pointed out that, when Miss Longstaffe tries to milk him for a larger marriage settlement than she was promised or had a right to expect, he responds with a letter that is plainly written, straightforward, honest, and, even, perhaps, proud. In his dealings with Georgiana Longstaffe's father, Breghert is similarly straightforward and honest. What is seldom noted by the critics, however, is the easy and smooth way in which Breghert conforms to the novel's scheme of the slowly increasing decadence of society by merely being a Jew who wishes for material reasons to enter its ranks. Breghert's pursuit of Georgiana Longstaffe possesses no iota of romantic sentiment. She is clearly his ladder to a position. And while it may be commendable that he does not disguise the fact, the feelings Breghert expresses for the woman of his choice so violently conflict with those of the few real lovers of the novel — the muscular saint Roger, the weakling Paul, and the flawless Henrietta — that the author's distaste for the character cannot be ignored.

This distaste is revealed in physical descriptions as Trollope gives rein to his feelings about Jews. Breghert resembles both a butcher and a hair dresser: "He was a fat greasy man, good looking in a certain degree, about fifty, with hair dyed black, and beard and moustache dyed a dark purple colour. The charm of his face consisted in a pair of very bright black eyes, which were, however set too near together in his face for the general delight of Christians. He was stout; – fat all over rather than corpulent, – and with that look of command in his face which has become common to master-butchers, probably by long intercourse with sheep and oxen" (II, 91). The satirical intention of the passage is signified by the ironical reference to the "charm of his face" as a prefix to a description of a distinctly uncharming, perhaps even sinister, pair of eyes. The wit is then compounded by reference to Breghert's speech, his name and his accent. His first wife, he tells the alarmed Georgiana, "used to call me Ezzy" (II, 96). He continues to press her for a honeymoon day as follows: "Vy not, my dear? Ve would (sic) have our little holiday in Germany" (II, 96). These details, relatively insignificant though they are in the novel as a whole, take on importance when applied to the larger construction of Melmotte. For they add details to a canvas in which the villain looms so large as to all but overwhelm everything else in it. The decadence of the "Now" alluded to in the title derives from a kind of new imperialism by which the mother country is being conquered, occupied, taken over by dark forces from without. These forces are introducing a poison into the system exemplified by the hopelessly outdated Roger Carbury who, almost alone in Britain, recognizes the foreign dirt threatening to soil his nation and says so. While it is undoubtedly true that Americans are also a part of this invasion of Britain, the novel's real ire is reserved for the Jews, whose presence in social, political, and intellectual positions of power truly menaces the nation. The Americans, after all, have America to go back to; their invasion of Britain is a form of plunder and retreat. The Jews are in Britain to stay. Their origins are always left obscure – vaguely European, probably German – a fact that reminds us of their essential homelessness and their amenableness to permanently locating amongst "us." But, Trollope keeps insisting, they can be recognized by their appearance – eyes, nose, hair, jaw – and by something ineffable which operates upon the sensibilities of their observers. Even Breghert, as seen in the above quotation, possesses a look of command which is common to the look of master butchers. The specific thing – the look – is deprived of specific shape by reference to a type of thing, a generalized look. Because Breghert is not a master butcher, all we can tell from the description is that he looks masterful and commanding in a way that the author clearly disapproves of and begrudges.

The novel is littered with minor Jewish characters whose doings add to the composite which Trollope is trying to construct. There is a Jew called Goldsheiner who, though he never enters the story except through gossip, is an example of a Jewish upstart who has married into an aristocratic family. While the following passage refering to Goldsheiner cannot be said to represent the author's views, it acts to release tension with the word "Jew" beating like a bell throughout. It is as though some subliminal anger is being released by the obsessive reiteration. The thoughts belong to Georgiana Longstaffe who is pondering her marriage to Breghert, and the sentiments are hers. But there seems to be a kind of relish in the author's use of the word; it suggests he is hiding behind his character's mean and narrow mind to let loose a flood of consciously self-demeaning resentment:

The man was absolutely a Jew; – not a Jew that had been, as to whom there might possibly be a doubt whether he or his father or his grandfather had been the last Jew of the family; but a Jew that was. So was Goldsheiner a Jew, whom Lady Julia Start had married, – or at any rate had been one a very short time before he ran away with that lady. She counted up ever so many instances on her fingers of 'decent people' who had married Jews or Jewesses. (II, 92)

So even the absent Goldsheiner is calumniated by the author, who makes him a ready convert to Christianity, thus supplying him with a base motive for his marriage and robbing him of all dignity in the process.

Another minor Jew in the novel is the sly, dishonest, and cowardly Samuel Cohenlupe, member of parliament for Staines, "a gentleman of the Jewish persuasion" (I, 84). Cohenlupe's function is to support Melmotte in concealing his financial crimes and then, at the end, to betray everyone by running away from England when trouble begins to loom. Through his name and title, the Jew-wolf from the befouled borough, Trollope suggests a kind of violent and sly rapacity.

Augustus Melmotte, on the other hand, is one of the towering Jews of English literature. For all his dislike of Jews, a dislike scattered liberally through his works, Trollope has created a

villain of truly massive dimensions in the person of Melmotte,
as only Shakespeare before him had done. The Jewish villains
in the works of Marlowe and Charles Dickens are one-dimensional in their evil so that their humanity is all but effaced.
Melmotte, like Shylock, possesses a kind of intestinal power
that is more than merely a function of his intelligence, though
it partakes of that too. Melmotte and Shylock are both passionate characters who, in mastering their passions, reveal the
source of their power to be the conflict of warring elements
within them. Their strength is a kind of aura flowing from an
inner contention. Shylock expresses this mastery through a viciously biting wit whose point is often too subtle for even his
fellow Venetians and which, consequently, gives him a kind of
secret amusement at their expense. Melmotte expresses power
through a rough, abrupt, terseness which conveys a sense of his
contempt for those around him. This contempt, in turn, has the
effect of convincing his acolytes of his strength. For all of Trollope's hatred of what Melmotte stands for, and for all of Trollope's dislike of Melmotte's inherently "Jewish" character, he
allows the character a natural growth refusing to succumb to
the solutions of melodrama and sensation which Dickens had
so egregiously done with Fagin. Melmotte's rough contempt is
shown in his conflict over the dictates of social decorum and his
propensity for physical violence. The power that others see in
Melmotte, in his looks and his carriage and his occasionally
slovenly restlessness, derives from an evident desire to crush
and tear down what stands before or around him. His brutishness is shown in several ways. For example, Melmotte is repeatedly associated with immensity of size as well as
monstrosity. He is a "gigantic swindler," who is rumoured to
have "swallowed up the property of all who had come into contact with him [and] was fed with the blood of widows and children" (I, 68). Though Trollope places such accusations into the
realm of gossip early in the novel, later, when Melmotte's fortunes are beginning to ebb, the character himself reflects on
having been "imprisoned for fraud at Hamburg," (I, 68). Thus
he lends credibility to the assertions that he is a bloodsucker
and that the gossip about his swindles on the continent are based
in truth. Mrs Hurtle who, for all her unladylikeness possesses
a ready eloquence, convincingly constructs a Melmotte whose
power and boldness place him beyond the standards by which
ordinary mortals are judged. She tells Paul Montague, "People
have said that Napoleon was a coward, and Washington a traitor.

You must take me where I shall see Melmotte. He is a man whose hand I would kiss; but I would not condescend to speak even a word of reverence to any of your Emperors ... Here is a man who boldly says that he recognizes no such law; that wealth is power and that power is good, and that the more a man has of wealth the greater and the stronger and the nobler he can be" (I, 246). Melmotte's heroic proportions are bolstered by such disinterested admiration; they are confirmed again and again, even in passages of invective against him, where the sheer venom argues the efficacy of his ability to affect the life of the nation. Roger Carbury's dismissal of Melmotte as "dirt in the gutter," (I, 138) deriving as it does from knowledge of the man only through his reputation, bespeaks the extent of his prejudice – a prejudice manifested by the willingness of a man who professes contempt for gossip to be so moved by it. The rise of Melmotte to prominence and power is concomitant with the increasing use of metaphorical language which describes his expanding physical and political presence in order, no doubt, that his fall might be the more widely felt. But, as he increases in prosperity and power, the sheer brutishness of his nature comes closer to the surface, until, towards the end of the novel, he is portrayed more in physical terms, his story increasingly defined by physical actions, while the abstractions of money and power fade into the background. As he rises, Trollope writes, "Augustus Melmotte was becoming greater and greater in every direction – mightier and mightier every day" (I, 323). Such words employed about a physically large man draw attention to the character's appearance without actually suggesting that he is physically expanding. "He was learning to despise mere lords and to feel that he might almost domineer over a duke" (I, 323).

The violence and monstrosity of Melmotte's character, while not overtly attributed to his being Jewish, derives from two sources. First, the novel is uncompromising in associating Jews with rough vulgarity and sharp practice. The only Jew in the novel who has a shred of humanity or dignity – Breghert – is depicted as being almost physically unacceptable to society. His physical presence disgusts almost all those who are permitted in the novel to discuss it – we never know, for example, how his children or friends regard him as a physical creature. The other Jews are either ugly or crooked; they all represent some kind of monstrous deformity in society, a deformity that, for the sake of the novel's larger purpose, indicates the increasing deformity of society. This is a moral schema into which

Melmotte fits comfortably. He is a large, unattractive man with a rather frightening demeanour and the manners of a bully.

Second, Melmotte performs two violent actions which, while not specifically associated with his Jewishness, tend to reinforce Trollope's conceptualization of it. As his fortunes are ebbing, Melmotte gets rid of some papers which, presumably, would condemn him if found. He burns the documents and scatters their ashes in the yard, but one document "he put bit by bit into his mouth, chewing the paper into a pulp till he swallowed it" (II, 119). The dynamic of that moment in the scene is enhanced by its brevity. Having swallowed the paper, Melmotte goes about his other business. Yet the reader is left with the shocking impression of this action, an impression whose power derives from the sheer unnaturalness and illogic of this act, which seems to indicate a violence turned against Melmotte. This is, of course, far from an act of cannibalism, but it may bring to mind Rumour's metaphorical charge against Melmotte that he had been fed upon the blood of widows and children. This may, in turn, bring to the reader's mind the charges of cannibalism and ritual slaughter levelled against Jews elsewhere in English literature. Trollope tantalizes us by not offering a reason why Melmotte consumes the paper. There is, also, a kind of penance implied in the action, a mortification of the flesh for Melmotte's failure; eating the paper brings Melmotte to an intense resolve never to betray himself "by the working of a single muscle, or the loss of a drop of blood from his heart. He would go through it, always armed without a sign of shrinking" (II, 119).

This act of violence, which momentarily dislocates the steady flow of dénouement, seems almost a therapy for adversity. Later is to come the most violent of all acts in the novel: Melmotte's vicious physical attack against the one person who cares nothing for his power and who refuses to bow to his will, his daughter Marie. Having attempted unsuccessfully to elope with the worthless Sir Felix Carbury, thus infuriating her father, Marie compounds her unfiliality by refusing to sign over money that had been put in her name as a safeguard. Her father attempts to reason with her, calming himself by a supreme effort of will. Then, when reason fails, he belabours his daughter viciously, with no success. The process is significant, and the implications are resonant. Melmotte's violent rage against his daughter leading to an actual attack upon her is reminiscent of Shylock's frantic and furious cry, "Would I had my daughter hearsed at my foot and my ducats in her ear." Though Melmotte has a wife, she is not the mother of his daughter; like Jessica therefore, she is a motherless girl who elopes (unsuccessfully in this case) with a Christian lover, who like Sir Felix, is attempting to make his fortune by the elopement. Each betrayal – Jessica's and Marie's – represents a flight to a better world than the daughters presently endure. And in each case the consequences are violently wrathful fathers, though only Melmotte is permitted to exact a violent punishment against the daughter who has robbed him.

As Melmotte prepares to use violence against his daughter, a kind of physical transformation takes place whereby his brutality becomes etched on his features: "The lower jaw squared itself, and the teeth became set, and the nostrils of his nose became extended – and Marie began to prepare herself to be 'cut to pieces'" (II, 254). The villainy of the attack is exacerbated by Trollope's quotation from Medea, the unresisting, silent, but tearless response of Marie herself, and the author's declaration that the scene of the beating is best left undescribed – "Nor will I attempt to harrow my readers by a close description of the scene which followed. Poor Marie! That cutting her up was commenced after a most savage fashion. Marie crouching down hardly uttered a sound. But Madame Melmotte frightened beyond endurance screamed at the top of her voice, – 'Ah, Melmotte, *tu la tueras!*'" (II, 257). To emphasize the viciousness of this beating, Trollope has provided an equivalent in the novel. When the working-class woman Ruby Ruggles refuses to obey her grandfather's wish that she accept John Crumb, he sets upon her. But here Trollope allows his English labourer an excuse, a justification that makes him less culpable than Melmotte. Ruggles is acting on behalf of the future good of his granddaughter, for whom this alliance offers no personal advantage. Ruby is less innocent than Marie Melmotte, in Trollope's eyes she is something of a promiscuous flirt. Marie Melmotte's notions of rising above her station through marriage to a baronet proclaim a kind of culpable stupidity. (We might note that Sir Felix Carbury is the cause of two innocent girls being beaten by men.) Finally, the clearest justification given Daniel Ruggles is that, unlike Melmotte, he is not entirely responsible for his actions: "But for the gin which he had taken he would hardly have struck her" (I, 318). Melmotte, who is damned thoughout the novel for not being a gentleman, and, certainly, for not being an Englishman, is starkly revealed through his violent abuse of his daughter. This act fulfills the threat of Shylock and partially reenacts the crime of Marlowe's Barabas. The child-killing Jew of my-

thology takes form in the person of this violent parent. Trollope
is referring, in this scene, to a construction of the Jew that is
part of the anti-Semite's history: the Jew is a ruthless monster
capable of unnatural acts of violence. Barabas, Shylock, Fagin,
– all possess this immense capacity for cruelty and destruction.
Indeed, Trollope used the idea in another scene involving Lopez, the Jewish villain of *The Prime Minister*. In this case Lopez's
blameless wife almost inspires her husband to strike her.

For all his anti-Semitism, Trollope betrays, in *The Way We
Live Now*, a nagging admiration for his Jewish villain. I have
mentioned an ambiguous element in his portrayal which seems
to derive from a recognition of the sheer intestinal power of
Melmotte. Even in the first description of the character there
is a strength which manifests itself in a propensity to bully and
a carelessness about Melmotte's essential vulgarity. But the
strength will assist Melmotte greatly when he prepares for death
by his own hand, after all attempts at self salvation have failed.
The author describes the suicide in terms of the demise of a
noble Roman: "But even he, with all the world now gone from
him with nothing before him but the extremest misery which
the indignation of offended laws could inflict, was able to spend
the last moments of his freedom in making a reputation at any
rate for audacity. It was thus that Augustus Melmotte wrapped
his toga around him before his death!" (II, 316) Trollope's ambiguity to his Jewish villain is heightened by giving Melmotte
the name and garb of a Roman emperor at his death.

It is a matter of curiosity that Trollope chooses to dispose of
his worst Jews, Melmotte and Lopez, by having them kill themselves in quasi-heroic fashion. There is no moral or dramatic
commeuppance accorded these two vicious characters in their
last moments. Rather, Trollope steps away from the action to
allow each character an ultimate privacy. Their minds made up,
their dignity intact or recovered, Melmotte and his young un-
derstudy, Lopez, approach death unflinchingly. Even in death
Melmotte exudes unbridled arrogance combined with a powerful assertion of will. His clear-eyed approach to dying causes
a change in the attitude towards him by author, reader, and his
friends and enemies alike: he becomes an object of sympathy
and admiration after having enjoyed antithetical responses
throughout the novel. Trollope's profound racial dislike of his
villain does not compel him to efface his humanity. This is, by
no means, a plea by Trollope for racial or religious toleration.
The novel continues to insist upon the social and moral crimi-
nality of Jews, though it allows them human feelings. The Jews

are damned throughout the novel, however, for their propensity to manipulate financial figures, for their ruthlessness in swindling, for their essential lack of finer feelings, for their inexcusable desire to enter society, for the obscurity of their origins, and for their lack of a place to which to return.

Melmotte's death is a huge release for society, as well as his own daughter. Society is relieved of having to soil its hands on him in exacting revenge; it is saved from the Jewish menace by the self-destruction of its most pernicious figure and by the retirement from the field of the lesser figures Cohenlupe and Breghert. Though it can hardly be said that the novelist allows a general absolution, there is in the conclusion a sufficiency of moral recovery by "deserving" characters to suggest a respite from the danger of a Jewish takeover and to propose a qualified optimism about the future possibility of a harmonious social order. Even Breghert, whom critics like to see as the salvageable Jew, makes no further attempts to enter British society, and is presumably permitted to return to his slightly greasy work of making money because he, at least, is honest about it. Cohenlupe, the crooked MP from Staines – a Jewish district whose name must have delighted Trollope – runs away to the continent where he belongs, with the other foreigners.

Trollope adds little to the prevailing idea of the Jew. His Jews fulfill the extant expectations developed by the stereotype. However, the very existence of a portrait such as that of Melmotte, with its lucidly delineated moral overtones, contributes to the tradition by which the notion becomes a received truth and augments the hold which the notion exerts over recipients of its "truth" – Trollope's public. The novel is a point of intersection for a great diversity of socially constructed assumptions. That some contradictions should emerge from the intersection is surely inevitable. For example, we cannot but note the contradiction between the vulgarity, greasiness, and butcherliness of Breghert and the "manly," straightforward, and grammatically impeccable letter he writes to Georgiana. Or the contradiction between the denigration of Melmotte as a swindling, ruthless monster of depravity and his genuine fortitude and true charisma. But in attempting to identify the source of these and other contradictions we are unavoidably led back to the unhelpful realm of biography, where our knowledge of the author can never be truly sufficient to provide the explanation we seek. We need, ultimately, to satisfy ourselves with the irremediable inadequacy of our knowledge and the inevitability of the contradiction.

CHAPTER FIVE

Jews and Women in George Eliot's Daniel Deronda

DEBORAH HELLER

In 1876 George Eliot, who was then the foremost English novelist of her day, published her last novel, *Daniel Deronda*, of which at least half is concerned with Jewish subjects. The hero of what has come to be referred to as "the Jewish half" of George Eliot's novel is Daniel Deronda, a young man who, having been raised by a British baronet to the life of an English gentleman in total ignorance of his Jewish parentage, gravitates improbably towards his own people. Deronda is presented in a wholly favourable, in fact, idealized light, as are other key Jews in the novel. There is, for example, Mirah, the virtuous young woman with whom Daniel falls in love, who is searching for her mother (who turns out to be dead) and brother. And there is that brother, Ezra Mordecai, who though but a humble watchmaker lodging with the family of a Jewish pawnbroker, is nonetheless presented as an inspired prophet along Old Testament lines. Mordecai's very speech – exalted, imagistic, not to say overloaded and turgid – is meant to suggest his intimate closeness to sources of prophetic and poetic genius, while his physiognomy, we are told on his first appearance, "might possibly have been seen in a prophet of the Exile, or in some New Hebrew poet of the medieval time."[1] Mordecai, who is dying, is wasting in body, yet his intensely vital spirit dreams of finding a handsome and healthy successor into whom he may pour his ardent imaginative vision of a revived and revitalized Jewish homeland in Palestine. He fastens on Deronda, despite the latter's denial (due to honest ignorance) of Jewish origins; nevertheless, Deronda, out of some almost mystical blood impulse, responds to Mordecai's intellectual charisma and begins, "in deference to Mordecai," (466) and out of his love for Mirah, whom he has rescued from drowning, to study things Jewish, to visit synagogues, and to learn Hebrew. Accompanied by Mordecai, Deronda spends an evening at a club of working-class Jews. This provides the occasion for a lengthy and, for its day, topical discussion of the pros, cons, and desired degrees of assimilation, as Mordecai's British co-religionists argue against his loftily phrased and often muddily verbose championing of what today we would call the Zionist ideal.

Written some twenty years before Theodore Herzl's *Der Judenstaat*, while Herzl was still a student in Vienna, *Daniel Deronda* is "reported to have played a considerable part in predisposing certain elements of European Jewry in favour of a Zionist movement."[2] In 1948 George Eliot had a street named after her in Tel-Aviv, and there are now streets named after her in all of Israel's major cities.[3]

As *Daniel Deronda* was to be much cherished by Zionists, so were George Eliot's contemporary Jewish readers much pleased with it. George Eliot was especially gratified by the praise she received from educated Jews for her accurate and extensive knowledge of Jewish history, literature, and customs.[4] However, during the writing of *Daniel Deronda*, both George Eliot and George Henry Lewes, her common-law husband, literary advisor, and agent, had their doubts about the way in which the British public would receive the Jewish half of the novel. Lewes wrote to George Eliot's publisher, John Blackwood, on 1 December 1875: "Your admiration is very cheering to her, and I must add that your taking so heartily to the Jewish scenes is particularly gratifying to me, for I have sometimes shared her doubts on whether people would sufficiently sympathize with that element in the story."[5] A letter from Blackwood to George Eliot on 7 September 1876 perhaps captures the general response of the English readership: "It is almost impossible to make a strong Jewish element popular in this country and it was perfectly marvelous to see how in your transitions [between the Jewish and English parts] you kept your public together. Anti-Jews grumbled but went on." On 12 October Lewes wrote to a friend: "we have both been much gratified at the fervent admiration of the Chief Rabbi and other learned Jews, and their astonishment that a Christian should know so much about them and enter so completely into their feelings and aspirations. This is all the more welcome because the Christian public – at least a large part of it – is decidedly unsympathetic towards that part of D.D." And on 29 October Lewes wrote to Blackwood: "The

Jews seem to be very grateful for Deronda – and will perhaps make up for the deadness of so many Christians to that part of the book which does not directly concern Gwendolen. When the cheap edition is issued we shall perhaps see the effect of this Jewish sympathy."

George Eliot herself wrote to Blackwood a few days later (3 November), "I expected to excite more resistance of feeling than I have seen the signs of," but Lewes, who followed George Eliot's reviews more closely than she did herself, may have made the more accurate assessment: "There seems to be so general a sense of disappointment – so much deadness to the Jewish element – that my only hope for a large sale until the public has learned to get over its first disappointment is in the Jewish public and they can only, I fear, be caught by the cheap edition" (22 November). Blackwood's reply reads: "The Jews should be the most interesting people in the world, but even *her* magic pen cannot *at once* make them a popular element in a Novel." George Eliot's Journal entry of 1 December conveys a sense of the mixed public response, accompanied, however, by indication of substantial sales, "an unmistakable guarantee that the public has been touched."

Although George Eliot and Lewes attributed the lack of enthusiasm for the Jewish part of the novel to the public's lack of sympathy for Jews in general, it is hard for us, at this distance, not to feel that this response must have also owed something to aesthetic considerations. In the century or so since the publication of *Daniel Deronda* there has been critical consensus that the Jewish half of the novel is, when judged simply on artistic grounds, not as good as the English half. While the English part is praised for its irony and its psychological and social subtlety and realism, the Jewish part has been uniformly faulted for its stiffness, didacticism, and idealization. In a contemporary review Henry James wrote, "All the Jewish part is at bottom cold,"[6] and more recently F.R. Leavis deplored the same unsatisfactory effect, while suggesting however that the problem was just the opposite – that the Jewish part suffered from an excess of emotional involvement by the author, from its not being sufficiently under her artistic control; as Leavis put it, Deronda is "a mere emotionalized postulate,"[7] and his suggestion that the novel would be better served by expunging the "bad" or Jewish half all together, leaving only the English portion which he would re-entitle *Gwendolen Harleth*,[8] provided the basis for much critical discussion. Barbara Hardy, while recognizing the thematic interrelatedness of the two sections of the book, has also complained about the difference in their modes of treatment, and faulted the hero for his artistic "lifelessness" and "absence of personality."[9] Edgar Rosenberg, summing up nearly a century of criticism, found the case against the Jewish half "unfortunately ... unarguable."[10]

This situation may sound familiar to readers acquainted with other one-dimensional "good Jews" in literature, such as Dickens's Mr Riah in *Our Mutual Friend*. Fundamental to the tradition of the "good Jew" is that an author's noble intentions inhibit his realism. Negative stereotypes, it is thought, can best be counteracted by positive stereotypes. Yet without denying the critical consensus which holds that George Eliot's virtuous Jews fail to achieve the multi-dimensional complexity of her most successful characters in *Daniel Deronda* and elsewhere, we still might pause to observe that her positive Jewish types celebrate a rather different set of virtues from the familiar ones of charity, humility, financial probity, and long-suffering patience that are typically exemplified by what one critic has called the "anti-Shylock" type in English literature.[11] Exactly which virtues George Eliot singles out as characteristically Jewish is something we shall return to shortly. I shall also argue that the generally held view that "the portrayal of Jewish society is almost entirely approving"[12] is something of an overstatement. On the simplest level, George Eliot makes use of negative as well as positive Jewish stereotypes. Beyond that, she suggests an awareness of the position of women in Jewish culture and tradition that is questioning, if not actually critical. For in the character of the hero's mother, who conforms to no pre-established stereotype, George Eliot has created an uncharacteristic, independent, talented, angry, "unfeminine," "modern" woman, who is in rebellion against the constraints imposed on her by traditional Judaism and the role it allots to women; and while she is by no means held up as a model, her undeniable charisma and eloquence help to make the traditional "feminine" submissive virtues of the apparently idealized Jewish heroine, Mirah, appear questionable indeed.

Before focusing more closely on the novel itself, however, it may be helpful to consider a few aspects of its background. The dominant philosemitism of *Daniel Deronda* was not always George Eliot's attitude. Some eighteen years before this last novel, commenting in a letter on the romanticized, idealized, prophetic Jewish leaders who were triumphant by virtue of their racial superiority in the novels of Benjamin Disraeli, George Eliot expressed her distaste for Disraeli's theory of the racial superiority of Jews and also for much of Judaism itself:

The fellowship of race, to which D'Israeli exultingly refers the munificence of Sidonia, is so evidently an inferior impulse which must ultimately be superseded that I wonder even he, Jew as he is, dares to boast of it. My Gentile nature kicks most resolutely against any assumption of superiority in the Jews, and is almost ready to echo Voltaire's vituperation. I bow to the supremacy of Hebrew poetry, but much of their early mythology and almost all of their history is utterly revolting. Their stock has produced a Moses and a Jesus, but Moses was impregnated with Egyptian philosophy and Jesus is venerated and adored by us only for that wherein he transcended or resisted Judaism. The very exaltation of their idea of a national deity into a spiritual monotheism seems to have been borrowed from the other oriental tribes. Everything *specifically* Jewish is of a low grade. (11 February 1848)

Although she was never to subscribe to Disraeli's mystic-racial theories, George Eliot's attitude to the Jews, obviously enough, did undergo a dramatic change, as the appreciative and heavily researched *Daniel Deronda* shows. Her lengthiest written comment on the didactic intention behind her last novel is found, fittingly, in a famous letter to Harriet Beecher Stowe, the American novelist whose *Uncle Tom's Cabin* had done so much to rouse public indignation against the evil of slavery. Stressing Christianity's moral and historical debt to Judaism and deploring the ignorant and contemptuous attitude toward Jews prevalent among her fellow Christians, George Eliot explained that she "therefore felt urged to treat Jews with such sympathy and understanding as my nature and knowledge could attain to ... I find men educated at Rugby supposing that Christ spoke Greek. To my feeling, this deadness to the history which has prepared half our world for us, this inability to find interest in any form of life that is not clad in the same coat-tails and flounces as our own lies very close to the worst kind of irreligion. The best that can be said of it is, that it is a sign of the intellectual narrowness – in plain English, the stupidity, which is still the average mark of our culture." (29 October 1876)

George Eliot's personal interest in Jews probably dates back

to her 1854 visit to Germany with Lewes, during which he had
introduced her to prominent Jews in the artistic, musical, and
scientific circles in which he was at home.[13] She subsequently
wrote a seminal article on the German Jewish writer Heinrich
Heine (1856), which set the dominant tone in British and American criticism for regarding Heine as the true successor of
Goethe in German literature,[14] a position he does not hold, incidentally, in German criticism, however standard this view of
him has become in Anglo-American letters. Her interest in Judaism and Jewish nationalism was given a certain personal impetus by her friendship with Emanuel Deutsch, an impassioned
believer in a Jewish homeland in Palestine, whom she met in
1866, who gave her weekly lessons in Hebrew and served as a
model for the dying Mordecai.[15] George Eliot's interest in Judaism should also be understood as part of her long-standing
interest in religion and religious history. In her youth George
Eliot (then Mary Ann Evans) went through a period of devout
commitment to Evangelical Protestantism, and one of the early
projects she conceived was to compile a chart of ecclesiastical
history. Among the translations she did before she came to write
fiction were not only Strauss' *Life of Jesus*, but also Spinoza's
Tractatus Theologico-Politicus as well as his *Ethics*.[16] Like many
Victorians she lost her faith, but she never abandoned her interest in religion or her respect for the capacity of the religious
life – or its moral equivalent – to counteract the narrow egoism
of our personal lot by offering a pattern for the transcendence
of self, for the dedication of the individual spirit to something
higher than mere self-interest. Achieving this transmutation of
self through submergence in some kind of higher, more significant, identity is a major theme in all of George Eliot's fiction.

Of equal and related thematic importance is the issue of moral
and spiritual guidance, though the guides who emerge in George
Eliot's novels are only sometimes religious leaders as well. But
we should not forget that her first published stories, subsequently collected under the title *Scenes of Clerical Life*, all had
clergymen heroes, and clergymen of one kind or another – including Savanarola, whose extended historical portrait appeared in *Romola* – figure prominently and largely sym-
pathetically in all her novels. In creating Daniel and Mordecai,
then, both of whom are conceived as specifically religious as
well as moral leaders, George Eliot is, in part, simply giving a
Jewish context to concerns that have been present in her fiction
all along. The visionary Mordecai, a spiritual guide who is at-

tempting to awaken his people to their wider, historical destiny, may fail with the Jewish workmen at the *Hand and Banner*, but he succeeds in preparing Deronda to accept the revelation of his Jewish birth in a spirit of joy, gratitude, and dedication to the future. Deronda himself is presented as the model of a political-spiritual leader, a kind of latter-day Moses. Yet he is ultimately to enact his political leadership only off-stage, so to speak, in the post-novelistic future, after he and his bride Mirah have sailed off the final pages and on to Palestine. What we see in the course of his education within the novel is the development of his wide sympathies and his desire to subordinate himself to some goal vaster than himself that will take the shape of duty. Through his love for Mirah and the discovery of his parents' identities he is blest by having "the very best of human possibilities ... befall him – the blending of a complete personal love in one current with a larger duty" (685).

Wide sympathies are always a virtue in George Eliot's world; the very words "wide" and "large" are key positive terms and are used repeatedly to characterize Deronda, in whom, for example, "there had sprung up ... a meditative yearning after wide knowledge" (217). But before he learns the secret of his birth, this virtue has been carried to excess and is in danger of becoming a fault. Until Daniel is made aware of his origins and his heritage, he is unable to determine his future, and he senses a disturbing aimlessness to his life.

His early-awakened sensibility and reflectiveness had developed into a many-sided sympathy, which threatened to hinder any persistent course of action ... His plenteous, flexible sympathy had ended by falling into one current with that reflective analysis which tends to neutralize sympathy ... what he most longed for was either some external event, or some inward light, that would urge him into a definite line of action, and compress his wandering energy ... But how and whence was the needed event to come? – the influence that would justify partiality, and making him what he longed to be yet was unable to make himself – an organic part of social life, instead of roaming in it like a yearning disembodied spirit, stirred with a vague social passion, but without fixed local habitation to render fellowship real? (412–13)

George Eliot holds to an organic view of individual human nature as of the wider social fabric. The healthy life, whether individual, social, or political, depends upon maintaining a vital connection between past, present, and future.[17] Thus Daniel, reflecting on his ignorance of his origins, hopes for "a disclosure which would hold the missing determination of his course," and help "him to make his life a sequence which would take the form of duty" (525,6). The very lack of personality that critics have seen in Daniel can be understood as psychologically appropriate to his having been kept in ignorance of his origins. It is almost as if he cannot become a full flesh and blood character until he is put in contact with his past – both his individual *and* his corporate, or racial and historic, past – which in turn will hold the key to determining his future. Deronda's plight is similar to accounts of adopted children who flounder and find it hard to move forward in life until they make contact with their natural parents. In Daniels' case, however, George Eliot is also making a wider social and political point.

Daniel Deronda, potential man of destiny, seeking submergence of his own identity in some higher duty and wider identification, is juxtaposed with Gweldolen Harleth, the brilliantly realized, self-centered heroine of the "English" half of the novel, whose desires at the outset range no farther than the fulfillment of her egoistic whims. George Eliot's imagery is always purposeful, and Gwendolen's narrowness is symbolized by her fear of wide spaces. "Solitude in any wide scene impressed her with an undefined feeling of immeasurable existence aloof from her, in the midst of which she was helplessly incapable of asserting herself" (94–5). Her narrow horizons are contrasted explicitly with the wide horizon of the world of art, in which she dabbles only as an amateur; when she is rebuffed for her singing at a social evening by the great musician Klesmer, she experiences "a sinking of heart at the sudden width of horizon opened round her small musical performance" (79).

In the development of this imagery Gwendolen is juxtaposed not only with Deronda but also with Mordecai, whose visionary, transcendent imagination is objectified by his love for far-stretching vistas.

He was keenly alive to some poetic aspects of London; and a favourite resort of his, when strength and leisure allowed, was to some one of the bridges, especially about sunrise or sunset. Even when he was bending over watch-wheels and trinkets, or seated in a small upper room looking out on dingy bricks and dingy cracked windows, his imagination spontaneously planted him on some spot where he had a far-stretching scene; his thought went on in wide spaces; and whenever he could, he tried to have in reality the influences of a large sky. (530)

Or again, "He yearned with a poet's yearning for the wide sky, the far-reaching vista of bridges" (537).

Though defined by a crippling narrowness that sharply contrasts her to the novel's two Jewish heroes, Gwendolen nonetheless turns to Deronda for moral and spiritual guidance following her disastrous marriage to a moral monster, Henleigh Grandcourt, a marriage through which she had naively and egoistically hoped to attain freedom and power. Deronda's counsel makes explicit the gulf between them: "Try to care about something in this vast world besides the gratification of small selfish desires" (502).

Gwendolen's upbringing as well as English society have encouraged both her narcissism and her constricting marriage — her rector-uncle having said of her suitor's proposal, in a kind of parody of Daniel's concern with duty, that the size of Grandcourt's fortune was such as "almost ... [to take] the question out of range of mere personal feeling, and ... [make] your acceptance of it a duty" (179). Throughout the novel, the materialism, philistinism, hypocrisy, and insular self-satisfaction of British society is contrasted with the idealism and wider culture and sympathy characteristic of the best elements of the Jewish section, and in this juxtaposition, as suggested earlier, English society emerges as morally flawed but wonderfully artistically realized, whereas the admirable Jewish elements are morally laudable but artistically unsatisfying. The final irony of this juxtaposition comes after Daniel has educted Gwendolen — who loves him and is now, opportunely, a widow — to fuller moral consciousness, only to announce to her his newly discovered Jewish identity and his plans to marry Mirah and sail for Palestine. "The world seemed getting larger round poor Gwendolen, and she more solitary and helpless in the midst. The thought that he might come back after going to the East, sank before the bewildering vision of these wide-stretching purposes in which she felt herself reduced to a mere speck" (875). Yet the irony is somehow unsatisfying, for England as well as Gwendolen is shown to be in desperate need of spiritual salvation, while the moral vitality that Daniel and the dream of Jewish renewal represent has, finally, as little relevance for the heroine as for her country. Just how England and Gwendolen are to be saved is a question that is implicit throughout the novel, and yet it is never adequately confronted or answered.

While this is the main pattern and principal juxtaposition in the novel, the foregoing account overlooks some much less favourable representatives of Judaism whose unattractiveness is inextricably tied to their conformity to familiar Jewish stereotypes. The pawnbroker Ezra Cohen with whom Mordecai lodges is a mildly repulsive portrait of Jewish vulgarity and self-satisfaction, though we are ultimately supposed to admire his domestic and religious devotion, his good-heartedness, and his business integrity. He is no worse, to be sure, than the satirized English – the Gascoignes, Mr Bult, the Arrowpoints – but whereas their satiric portrayals show wit and originality, Ezra Cohen is an identifiable stereotype who never surprises but only confirms; he defines himself on his first meeting with Deronda:

Well, sir, I've accommodated gentlemen of distinction – I'm proud to say it. I wouldn't exchange my business with any in the world. There's none more honourable, nor more charitable, nor more necessary for all classes, from the good lady who wants a little of the ready for the baker, to a gentleman like yourself, sir, who may want it for amusement. I like my business, I like my street, and I like my shop. I wouldn't have it a door further down. And I wouldn't be without a pawn-shop, sir, to be the Lord Mayor. It puts you in connection with the world at large. I say it's like the government revenue – it embraces the brass as well as the gold of the country. And a man who doesn't get money, sir, can't accommodate. (442)

And Ezra's young son Jacob on first meeting Deronda is instinctively ready to swap pocket knives: "'Have *you* got a knife?' says Jacob, coming closer. His small voice was hoarse in its glibness, as if it belonged to an aged commercial soul, fatigued with bargaining through many generations" (441).

The figure of the Jew pawnbroker/moneylender hovers as well at both ends of *Daniel Deronda*. Early on there is the dealer, Mr Wiener, to whom Gwendolen sells her turquoise necklace (which Deronda redeems); and near the end of the novel we learn the identity of Daniel's father through his widow's summary account stressing how he was so devoted to her that he "wound up his money-changing and banking, and lived to wait on me" (696). Unlike Ezra Cohen and his son, these peripheral figures are completely faceless and without personality. Their existence serves chiefly to confirm the "type," though the Leubrun pawnbroker is also there to establish the knee-jerk anti-Semitism from which Gwendolen (48), and, presumably, the reader, are to move in the course of the novel. George Eliot helps to orchestrate this movement by allowing both Gwendolen and the reader to assume initially that Deronda is a Christian, and by letting Deronda engage her and our sympathies before his true identity is known.

Much more distasteful than Ezra Cohen, his son, or the peripheral pawnbroker/moneylenders is Lapidoth, Mirah and Mordecai's delinquent father. He has been guilty of abducting Mirah from her mother and brother, of sending her on stage at an early age, and of scoffing at their religion which he does not practise. More despicable still, he has underhandedly contrived, for his own financial gain, to sell his daughter into concubinage with some foreign count, a situation considerably more loathsome than any of the marriages for social or financial advantage urged on daughters by the gentile English families, with which Lapidoth's intentions are sometimes too readily equated. No Christian parent in the novel reveals such crude greed or behaves as odiously toward an offspring as does Lapidoth – even the despicable Grandcourt shows more solicitude toward his children. Lapidoth does, however, provide the occasion for showing the filial virtue of Mirah and Mordecai, who are willing to take him in despite everything. Only because his uncontrollably (perhaps stereotypically Jewish?) thieving fingers cannot resist the temptation to pocket Deronda's ring does he opportunely disappear from the scene.

The evident purpose of these unattractive Jews is to balance, and therefore give credibility to, the more ideal Jews. What is distressing about them, however, is that their unattractiveness is automatically presented as having a peculiarly Jewish flavour, as conforming, in short, to pre-established negative stereotypes. Where Gwendolen's husband is one of the most original villains in English literature, Lapidoth is an identifiable Jewish villain, almost ready-made.

Comic Shylock though he be,[18] as an itinerant actor Lapidoth shows his kinship to the good Jews in the novel, who are presented not only in the roles of spiritual and political prophet, visionary and leader, exemplified by Mordecai and Deronda, but also as the representatives of almost all cosmospolitan and artistic values in the novel.[19] Almost all the Jews and certainly all the idealized Jews in the novel conform to the label popularized by Karl Marx – they are rootless cosmospolitans. The rising musical genius Klesmer is described as being "a felicitous combination of the German, the Sclave, and the Semite"[20] (77). In an exasperated response to a patronizing English philistine who asks whether Klesmer is a panslavist, the musician retorts, "No; my name is Elijah. I am the Wandering Jew" (284), a characterization that could apply with equal force to many of his coreligionists in the novel. In keeping with the imagery found elsewhere in the book, "Klesmer's personality," we are told, "especially his way of glancing round him, immediately suggested vast areas and a multitudinous audience" (539).

Deronda himself most fully exemplifies the rootless cosmopolitan position of the Jews, a position which, for the favourably treated characters in this novel, is inextricably bound up with their appreciation of wide intellectual horizons. The son of two Sephardic Jews, given by his mother after his father's death to Sir Hugo Mallinger to be raised as a British gentleman, Deronda nonetheless displays a "boyish love of universal history, which made him want to be at home in foreign countries" (220). After studying at Cambridge he chooses to complete his education abroad, explaining, "I want to be an Englishman, but I want to understand other points of view. And I want to get rid of a merely English attitude in studies" (224). It is while visiting a synagogue in Frankfurt that he is spotted by his grandfather's closest friend, Joseph Kolonymos; and later, after his meeting in Genoa with his mother (née Charisi but now the Princess Halm-Eberstein, wife of a Russian nobleman and bearing a German name), Deronda tells her, "I think it would have been right that I should have been brought up with the consciousness that I was a Jew, but it must always have been a good to me to have as wide an instruction and sympathy as possible" (725). Deronda's aspirations to wide-ranging, non-parochial knowledge and sympathy reflect the Enlightenment ideal of universal culture, while his need for roots, for a fixed local habitation, expresses the nineteenth-century respect for nationalism, for the particularized sense of national identity. Through his character more than any other, George Eliot is able to celebrate both impulses, while subsuming the eighteenth-century ideal within the predominant one of her own era.

Mirah and her brother were born in England. Their father's ancestors came from Poland, but he speaks German better than he speaks English. From England, Lapidoth takes Mirah to

New York, then to Hamburg, Vienna, and Prague, whence she flees to England. Mordecai, though born in England, is nourished in Holland at the feet of his uncle, a rabbi, but subsequently studies in Hamburg and Göttingen, "that I might take a larger outlook on my people, and on the Gentile world, and drink knowledge at all sources" (555).

In addition to their rootless cosmopolitanism, the Jews in *Daniel Deronda* are gifted artistically, especially as musicians. Lapidoth is a small-time actor, but, exploitive father though he be, he has managed to provide excellent instruction in singing and acting for his daughter, Mirah, who has an exquisite – though delicate – voice. Daniel, too, sings well as a boy, though he is shocked and offended when Sir Hugo asks if he would like to be a singer when he grows up. But Daniel's mother, like Klesmer, is a great artist, a talented singer-actress, known as "the Alcharisi" in the days of her international theatrical triumph. To be free to pursue her vocation in the face of her father's disapproval of an artistic career, she married her weak, adoring cousin, though she had not wanted to marry at all. After his death she married again, but only after she feared her voice had begun to go bad and her life as an artist had come to an end.

Deronda's mother, though she appears in only two late chapters, is to me one of the most interesting characters in the novel and in George Eliot's fiction as a whole. George Eliot's gallery of female characters contains a number of young women of exceptional sensibility, but none, with the exception of Dinah Morris in *Adam Bede*, seems to have any particular talent for a specific vocation, and Dinah's charismatic preaching is abruptly cut short by the new Methodist policy prohibiting women preachers. Typically, when these young women, such as Dinah or Dorothea Brooke (in *Middlemarch*), grow past early womanhood (as, for example, Maggie Tulliver of *The Mill on the Floss* does not) we are asked to accept that they find a qualified fulfillment of their exceptional natures through a happy marriage and motherhood. The Princess Halm-Eberstein is distinguished, first, by being George Eliot's only exceptional female character who has a concrete vocation at which she excels and which she pursues into adulthood. She is, in short, this great woman novelist's only major successful "career woman," as well as her only major woman artist. (Lydgate's first love, Laure, in

Middlemarch is an interesting early prototype, though she is more suggestive than developed.) She is also George Eliot's only portrait of a feminist figure.

The Princess Halm-Eberstein is a foil to Gwendolen, Mirah, and Daniel alike. Gwendolen, we are told early on, "Having always been the pet and pride of the household, waited on by mother, sisters, governess, and maids, as if she had been a princess in exile ... naturally found it difficult to think her own pleasure less important than others made it" (53). The refrain of Gweldolen as princess in exile is sounded several times, for example, "Always she was the princess in exile, who in time of famine was to have her breakfast-roll made of the finest bolted flour from the seven thin ears of wheat, and in a general decampment was to have her silver fork kept out of the baggage" (71). With a society girl's ability to sing a little and participate in a *tableau vivant*, Gwendolen, when fallen on hard times, fancies she might instantly make a living as an actress, only to be bitterly humiliated by Klesmer's unbiased judgment. Gwendolen has neither the talent nor the training of an artist; nor has she the discipline or temperament necessary to acquire such training. A princess in exile only by virtue of her own and her family's sense of her entitlement, she might even be said to conform to today's popular stereotype of the Jewish Princess, to whom somehow all shall be given and from whom nothing asked. However, Gwendolen stands in sharp contrast here to the real Jewish princess, the Princess Halm-Eberstein, who has willingly sought to sacrifice her life to her art, as well as to Mirah, who also recognizes art as a disciplined and serious calling.

Like Gwendolen, however, Deronda's mother married for freedom, which is never an admirable motive for George Eliot, who felt that virtue consisted, rather, in responding to the duties life confronted us with. And yet her quest for freedom appears less reprehensible than Gwendolen's, because although she sought freedom from the bondage of being a Jewish woman, an impulse George Eliot could hardly endorse, she also sought freedom to pursue the larger life of art, an expansive, non-egoistic motive which we are encouraged, at least to some extent, to admire. Again, in presenting Daniel's mother, George Eliot's language is revealing. The Princess Halm-Eberstein tells Daniel that, according to her father's view, "I was to care for ever about what Israel had been; and I did not care at all. I cared for the wide world and all that I could represent in it ...

I wanted to live a large life ... and be carried along in a great current." (693). Like the words "wide" and "large," "currents" are almost always good in George Eliot; to be carried along in a current often symbolizes the praiseworthy submergence of self in some higher, wider identity.

Thus, it is too simple to dismiss the princess as selfish, though in some sense she is this too, and too simple to dismiss her, as has been done, as the character "who most clearly articulates the position of the assimilationist,"[21] though in some sense she does do this as well. The striking point about her is that all that Daniel finds by embracing Judaism – large horizons, wide vistas, submergence in an existence greater than himself – his mother could find only by rejecting Judaism ("I cared for the wide world ... I wanted to live a large life"). The aspirations of mother and son are remarkably similar. Yet the fate of Deronda's mother serves to illustrate – whether intentionally or not – how very different are the roles, status, and options which Judaism offered to men and women. Speaking of her father, the princess tells Deronda:

I was to be what he called "the Jewish woman" under pain of his curse. I was to feel everything I did not feel, and believe everything I did not believe. I was to feel awe for the bit of parchment in the *mezuza* over the door; to dread lest a bit of butter should touch a bit of meat; to think it beautiful that men should bind the *tephillin* on them, and women not, – to adore the wisdom of such laws, however silly they might seem to me ... You are not a woman. You may try – but you can never imagine what it is to have a man's force of genius in you, and yet to suffer the slavery of being a girl. To have a pattern cut out – "this is the Jewish woman; this is what you must be; this is what you are wanted for; a woman's heart must be of such a size and no larger, else it must be pressed small, like Chinese feet; her happiness is to be made as cakes are, by a fixed receipt." That was what my father wanted. He wished I had been a son; he cared for me as a makeshift link. (692–3, 694)

While women today may find her ready assumption that "force of genius" is generally a masculine preserve to be somewhat offensive, as well as at odds with the dominant feminist spirit of her speech, it is important to recognize here that what the princess has rejected is not so much Judaism *per se* as the traditional role of the Jewish woman. Moreover, in not wanting to have her heart ... pressed small, like Chinese feet" the princess presents herself as a contrast to Mirah as well as to Gwendolen;

for Mirah, embodying an ideal of dutiful, unassertive – almost Dickensian – female virtue, is characterized not only by her "small" voice, but also by feet so small that even in the compact, doll's house-like abode of the diminutive Meyrick women, "there were no shoes in the house small enough for Mirah" (249).

In her speeches to Daniel the princess's passionate rage and hurt at the subordinate, constricting role allotted her as the Jewish woman seem scarcely to have abated through all the intervening years of artistic and social triumphs: "My father had tyrannised over me – he cared more about a grandson to come than he did about me: I counted as nothing. You were to be such a Jew as he; you were to be what he wanted" (698). Though she seems perplexed that the Jewish identity, which was bondage to her and from which she therefore thought to save her son, should come, instead, as liberation to him, this different response is entirely in keeping with her own account of the different roles offered to men and women by the religion she has rejected. Showing Daniel a portrait of herself in her youth she asks,

"Had I not a rightful claim to be something more than a mere daughter and mother? The voice and the genius matched the face. Whatever else was wrong, acknowledge that I had a right to be an artist, though my father's will was against it. My nature gave me a charter."

"I do acknowledge that," said Deronda, looking from the miniature to her face, which even in its worn pallor had an expression of living force beyond anything that the pencil could show. (728–9)

But in embracing Judaism Daniel will, of course, be much more than a "mere" son and father; he will have a vocation as well in political leadership, a legitimate outlet for *his* living force.

The subordinate position of women exists in the English as well as the Jewish part of the novel, of course. Gwendolen's tragic marriage comes about in part because social attitudes unanimously support her mother's reiterated contention that "Marriage is the only happy state for a woman" (58), and Gwendolen's aunt and uncle fully share her own disparaging view of her sisters, "it [was] a pity there were so many girls" (61). Gwendolen's cousin, Anna Gascoigne, the sister of "a brother whose pleasures apart from her were more than the sum total of hers" (87), feels herself "much at home with the Meyrick girls, who knew what it was to have a brother, and to be generally regarded as of minor importance in the world" (717). We learn, in another repeated refrain, that "Lady Mallinger felt apologetically about herself as a woman who had produced nothing but daughters in a case where sons were required" (267), and we see how social norms confirm her self-image "as the infelicitous wife who had produced nothing but daughters, little better than no children, poor dear things" (498). Far crueler than any of these instances is the outcast position of Grandcourt's cast-off mistress, Lydia Glasher, whose appearance in Gwendolen's life comes with the force of "some ghastly vision ... in a dream ... [saying] 'I am a woman's life'" (190). George Eliot certainly makes us aware of the injustice of the double standard governing society's very different treatments of Mrs Glasher and Grandcourt, who as a potential husband for Gwendolen is regarded quite genially by her rector uncle, Mr Gascoigne: "Whatever Grandcourt had done, he had not ruined himself; and it is well known that in gambling, for example, whether of the business or holiday sort, a man who has the strength of mind to leave off when he has only ruined others, is a reformed character" (125).

But while exposing these inequities, George Eliot's narrative *persona* never frontally challenges them. In fact, the tone with which woman's inferior status is treated throughout the English sections is urbane, ironic, at bottom one of resigned acceptance; it therefore differs radically from the princess's impassioned, angry, unforgiving outbursts, which are never mediated by any softening authorial comment. The irony and controlled satire characteristic of the English parts have, as indicated earlier, been contrasted to the emotional, idealizing treatment of the Jewish theme; in this contrast it is generally accepted (after Leavis) that George Eliot's more "mature" imagination was at work in the English sections and that her more "immature" emotionalism surfaced in the Jewish parts. In fact, more unconscious impulses may be revealed in the Jewish half of the novel than Leavis bothered to note. Which is, after all, the more "mature," "appropriate" perspective on the inferior status of women? Subdued irony, or impassioned rage?

We know, of course, that George Eliot did not consider herself a feminist. While approving of educational opportunities for women who could benefit from them (she gave fifty pounds toward the establishment of Girton College), and endorsing the Napoleonic ideal of "'La carrière ouverte aux talen[t]s,' whether the talents be feminine or masculine," she was dubious of many feminist causes, such as the enfranchisement of women, expressing the view that "woman does not yet deserve a much better lot than man gives her," and she repeatedly refused to undertake "specific enunciation of doctrine on a question so entangled as the 'Woman Question.'"[22] She could even state that the fact that "woman seems to me to have the worse share in existence" should be the "basis for a sublimer resignation in woman and a more regenerating tenderness in man."[23] It is hardly likely that she considered the princess's assault on the role of the Jewish woman powerful enough to vitiate the novel's dominant respectful and admiring attitude toward Jews, which was, after all, George Eliot's clear, conscious intent.

Indeed, one has to recognize a certain ambivalence of judgment, uncharacteristic of George Eliot, in her presentation of the princess. Certainly, any assessment of Deronda's mother has to accommodate the fundamentally disquieting fact of her having given her child to be raised by another, and of her admitted inability to love, both of which cannot help but qualify our sympathy with her, if not with her feminist indignation. Neither of these aspects of her experience, it should be said, is presented as particularly Jewish, and referring to them the princess deliberately extends her attack from the ideal of the Jewish woman to more widely diffused ideas about the uniform nature of womanhood itself:

Every woman is supposed to have the same set of motives, or else to be a monster. I am not a monster, but I have not felt exactly what other women feel – or say they feel, for fear of being thought unlike others. When you reproach me in your heart for sending you away from me, you mean that I ought to say I felt about you as other women say they feel about their children. I did not feel that. I was glad to be freed from you. But I did well for you, and I gave you your father's fortune. (691)

Although the princess may subtly be suggesting that her failure to find self-fulfillment in motherhood is less unusual than it appears, what remains unique about her, and prevents any easy generalization of her experience to that of other women, is her artistic gift, her "force of genius," which, as the conversation with Deronda implies, entitles her to claim a special privilege. At the same time, we must remember that the laws of poetic justice under which George Eliot usually operates suggest that the princess – whom we meet years after her glorious career has ended, as an unhappy, dying woman, driven by forces almost beyond her control to reveal to Deronda the secret of his birth which she had worked so hard to conceal – is, for all her eloquence and charisma, probably intended to be more judged than applauded.

Yet George Eliot was certainly aware of the subordinate position of women both in Victorian English society and in traditional Judaism, as of some of the differences between the two, and it may be that she found it easier to attack such subordination – or at least to allow one of her characters to attack it – when it appeared in an alien culture and when the attack was placed in the mouth of a character whom we are not, nominally, encouraged to approve. The white heat of the princess' unremitting resentment at the bondage imposed on her by her sexual identity is strikingly without parallel in any of George Eliot's other – and English – female characters.[24] George Eliot's awareness of the subordinate position of women in traditional Judaism finds its way into the novel in quiet, unobtrusive ways as well. One of the Meyric girls, for example, "who was much of a practical reformer" and has visited a synagogue with Mirah, "could not restrain a question. 'Excuse me, Mirah, but *does* it seem quite right to you that the women should sit behind rails in a gallery apart?'" (410). George Eliot herself had reported, interestingly, of one of her many visits to a synagogue, this one in Amsterdam: "in the evening we went to see the worship there. Not a woman was present, but of devout *men* not a few, curious reversal of what one sees in other temples."[25] And Ezra Cohen refers to the traditional Jewish prayer in which "a man is bound to thank God, as we do every Sabbath, that he was not made a woman; but a woman has to thank God that He has made her according to His will" (636) – a clear error on George Eliot's part (as an early Jewish critic point out), for this thanksgiving is in fact part of the *daily* morning prayer.

Although Daniel "will not say that I shall profess to believe exactly as my fathers have believed" (792), there is no suggestion that he has in mind revitalizing Judaism in any way that would affect the position of women or accommodate the princess's artistic and cosmopolitan aspirations. Daniel's chosen bride Mirah, with her preternaturally small feet, dismisses Amy Meyrick's question about the synagogue's revealing seating arrangement with the pious reply, "Yes, I never thought of anything else" (410), and willingly embraces the life of a Jewish woman. But both Gwendolen Harleth and the Princess Halm-Eberstein are more interesting and convincing women than Mirah, and neither can be so automatically "capable," as Daniel says of Mirah, "of submitting to anything in the form of duty" (617).

Daniel submits to a wider duty at the end, but, as I have suggested, it is clear that this duty offers him far greater scope than the duties of a Jewish daughter, wife, and mother, as presented in this novel, can offer any woman. As it appears in the novel, comparable human scope can be found by a Jewish woman only through denying her Jewishness; and this may suggest that when one ponders the role of Daniel's mother and the "Woman Question" in general in *Daniel Deronda*, the novel may emerge as somewhat less idealizing of Jewish life than it is generally taken – and was consciously intended – to be.

CHAPTER SIX

The Jew in
James Joyce's Ulysses

HARRY GIRLING

Unlike the Jews discussed in the previous chapters, the Jew in James Joyce's *Ulysses*, Leopold Bloom, is usually thought of as an Everyman figure. Not that he is going about looking for his soul, like the central character of the medieval play of *Everyman*. Rather he is like the man in the street, but larger and plumper than life; he is nothing and everything at the same time. He is a fairly faithful husband with a constant hankering towards an adulterous intrigue; he earns enough to get by, though he has to resort to various stratagems to stay afloat; he has quite good taste in music, but his chief interest in art is in trying to find out whether marble goddesses have a nether orifice; he has lots of acquaintances and no particular chums; he is fairly greedy and a bit fastidious; inclined to avoid trouble except when he is suddenly a hero; a father pining for a dead son who miraculously is endowed with a spiritual heir; a restless traveller who comes home as if he will never leave it again.

So the only remarkable thing about Leopold Bloom is that he is a Jew. Come to that, he is not much of a Jew at all, with neither a sense of Jewish lineage nor a Jewish upbringing. His father, not he, swallowed the bait of the Society for the Conversion of the Jews, gave up his religion and changed his name from Virag to Bloom. But Leopold knows himself to be, and is known as, a Jew in a nation – the Irish – and a society – Dublin – where Jews are few and are even said to be non-existent. His name is Jewish, his appearance is Jewish, and he himself, if the ragbag of his mind contained the material to say so, would not shrink from the final banality of claiming that he has a Jewish soul. Bloom is probably circumcised, for he was born when his father was still Jewish, though Joyce does not say so, not even when Bloom is admiring his own penis in the bathtub, "the limp father of thousands, a languid floating flower" (71).[1] The chief model for Leopold Bloom was a writer Joyce befriended in Trieste, Ettore Schmitz, an Italian Jew who published the delightful *Confessions of Zeno* under the pen name of Italo Svevo in 1923. Zeno is not a Jew; the chief quality he shares with Bloom is a charming incapacity for taking himself seriously.

We may wonder why James Joyce chose to make his man in the middle, the average sensual man, a Jew. There is no obvious answer. The reader may decide that Leopold Bloom epitomises, merely by his survival, the shifts and compromises that have controlled the lives of all the people in the twentieth century who have been so fortunate as to survive war and catastrophe – an emergence millions of Jews were cruelly deprived of. Bloom's journey through Dublin on a single day represents in some fashion the itinerary of a twentieth-century survival. Such a view does not take in anything resembling the holocaust, but who in the first quarter of the twentieth century would have dared to contemplate, in his most terrified imaginings, the horrors that the second quarter was to bring forth?

James Joyce's *Ulysses* was published by Shakespeare and Company in Paris on Joyce's fortieth birthday, 2 February 1922. Parts of the book, which he had been writing since 1914, had been published in periodicals from 1918 onwards. The publication history is a fascinating story of struggle against censorship and suppression, a struggle which ended in America after the epoch-making judgment given in the New York District Court by Justice Woolsey in October 1933 and the subsequent publication of the novel by Random House. The corresponding publication in Great Britain by John Lane did not take place until 1936.

These bare written-out dates – 1914, 1918, 1922, 1933, 1936 – cannot be thought of as mere figures. As we look back to 1933 and 1936 from the last decades of the twentieth century, we are aware of the gathering shadows that were soon to close upon Europe and the world, the darkness and tragedy of the Nazi attempt at world domination, and all the agony of the "final solution." The years 1914–18 bring to mind another kind of mass slaughter, another European tragedy, as devastating though not as evil as the Nazi destruction. Amid all these annals of doom it is difficult to come back to the date in the middle, the year 1922, and to find there some lights of hope shining, of which *Ulysses* was one.

We cannot expect to find euphoria in the years immediately after the ending of the European war in November 1918. The frantic rejoicing of Armistice Night in London marked the end of a universal disaster, but hard after came both every kind of local disaster and the influenza epidemic that claimed more victims than the war had done. Yet many people wanted to believe that the "war to end wars" would serve as a permanent warning to competing nations and that the Treaty of Versailles would establish permanent peace. In spite of all discouragements, until 1939 some idealists continued to hope that the nations could avoid war, believing in the League of Nations with a fervour that the United Nations Organization, with its cynical great-power share-out, never inspired.

One of the reasons for hope in the years after 1918 was that four great empires, the Russian, the Austrian, the Prussian, and the Ottoman, had all crumbled, dismantling some ancient fortresses of reaction and repression. Tsarist Russia had been the European example of institutionalized persecution of Jews. Anti-Semitism was everywhere, of course, but governmental authorization for it was more flagrant in Russia than elsewhere. It was Russia that made the world familiar with the word and the event *pogrom*, and not without reason were brutal police everywhere called "Cossacks." But can one say that the Tsarist anti-Semitism was worse than the Stalinist? One way in which it was better was that Jews were allowed to emigrate from the land of oppression, to flood across the Atlantic and also to other free countries round the world, there to establish the first durable form of the new Zion, part of which was the Lower East Side, New York.

The break-up of the old continental empires (which allowed the British, French, and American empires to acquire some new overseas colonies) liberated some national minorities that had aspired for centuries to become nations. The years after 1918 also saw several new states looking round them in new-found pride: Balkan states, Baltic states, Czecho-Slovakia, Poland, Hungary. They did not all become democratic havens of tolerance, but those that did lit up in a glory that was to prove desperately short-lived. Many lost their independence in 1939 or before, some betrayed by enemies, some by false friends such as those whose abandonment of Czecho-Slovakia made the war inevitable.

Two of the small states that achieved or advanced towards freedom after 1918 were Israel and Ireland. Israel had not moved very far towards statehood in 1922, but the essential

step had been taken: after the Balfour Declaration of 1917 prom-
ising a Jewish national home, the military defeat of Turkey en-
abled the League of Nations in 1922 to grant a mandate to Great
Britain to bring it about. Many years of difficulty and struggle
were to follow before the state of Israel was proclaimed on
15 May 1948, but the mandate of 1922 can be regarded as the
first hint of Zion – as Leopold Bloom calls it, "the golden city
which is to be, the new Bloomusalem" (395). Also in 1922, more
than two centuries of wrongs and self-sacrificing resistance
came to an end in Ireland when the Irish Free State was established by the ratification of a treaty with Great Britain on 8
January. The failed rebellion during Easter 1916 had made another fifteen martyrs for old Ireland, fifteen martyrs for the
Crown, as the ballad of Kevin Barry would put it; but this time
all the hanged men

Are changed, changed utterly:
A terrible beauty is born.

Although the poet, W.B. Yeats, did not mean it thus, the "terrible
beauty" was Irish freedom, born in 1922 after the years of
oppression. Ireland had suffered, from 1919 to 1921, the post-
war years of terrorism and counter-terrorism when the Black
and Tans, British mercenaries, fought the Irish Republican
Army. After the treaty, Ireland did not spend long on the arts
of peace. The civil war between the Free State Army and the
Irish Republican Army began in June 1922 (just after Joyce's
fortieth birthday and the publication of *Ulysses*). Irishman shot
Irishman until 1926, when the last guerilla fighters surrendered.
"Irelan' sober is Irelan' free" says Jack Boyle, drunker than ever,
at the end of Sean O'Casey's *Juno and the Paycock*. There is not
much possibility of Ireland becoming habitually sober (who
would wish it?); more than sixty years later there still seems
little possibility of Ireland becoming free of the shadow of a
gunman. For the last twenty years the civil war has moved to
Ulster, and Irishmen shoot Irishmen not because they are "die-
hards" or "staters" but because they are Catholics or Protestants. And who can say when the shooting will end in the golden
city of Zion?

– But it's no use, says [Bloom]. Force, hatred, history, all that. That's
not life for men and women, insult and hatred. And everybody knows
that it's the very opposite of that that is really life.
– What? says Alf. (273)

What? indeed. There is an answer, in one word, but it will be better to make further acquaintance with Leopold Bloom and with James Joyce before coming back to it.

The present task is to rediscover, looking back across all the horrors of the twentieth century, the "radical innocence" (Yeats's phrase) of the moment in 1922 when *Ulysses* was published, to discern in the novel the intertwined cord of Jewish freedom and Irish freedom, with the promise that any interest in Joyce's masterpiece is "self-delighting, self-appeasing, self-affrighting" (still Yeats) even if the focus is no more than the emerging portrait of a Jew. After all, those tourists (not few) whose only interest in foreign places is in seeking out the old synagogues – in Florence, Athens, Bombay – usually find some incidental entertainment in the streets they pass through on their way to the Jewish shrines.

Joyce made a brief statement about the purpose of his book when he sent an elaborate scheme of the episodes and their very rich system of symbolic equivalences to his friend Carlo Linati in 1920. "It is the epic of two races (Israel – Ireland) and at the same time the cycle of the human body as well as a little story of a day (life) ... It is also a kind of encyclopedia."[2]

Of all the ways in which *Ulysses* could be described, an "epic of two races (Israel – Ireland)" is not the most obvious. These threads are easily traced, but they are only strands in a total whose complexity, variety, subtlety, and fascination are beyond description. Though Joyce himself rejoiced in the layers of symbolism, the intricate correspondences, the constant cross-referencing, the wealth of historical detail, his intimate knowledge of Dublin streets and places, and above all the basic structuring of episodes from Homer's *Odyssey* – any admirer can spin out other comparisons and footnotes that are relevant and valuable – an interested reader can dispense with the whole apparatus of explanation and follow the story page by page. Some pages are transparently clear, some so obscure that no clues can help, some so perverse that they look like an elaborate leg-pull, and some so winning that the reader wants them to go on forever.

The preliminary indications given here do not amount to the elementary guidelines that are supposed to be necessary for a reading of *Ulysses*. No guidance of any kind is required. It is not even obligatory to read through from the beginning – the book may just as well be started anywhere in the middle. The few descriptive lines extracted below are meant to provide some continuity to the narrative, with the implicit assumption that Leopold Bloom, a genial soul, will introduce the reader to the glories of *Ulysses* and to the genius of James Joyce.

The three principal strands in the novel are the episodes from Homer's *Odyssey*, the succession of events in a single day in Dublin, and the coming together of the two principal characters, Leopold Bloom and Stephen Dedalus. Each of these strands runs through the whole narrative, and each forms an independent pattern by which the whole novel could be followed.

Ulysses was a leader in the Greek army which besieged Troy for ten years. As if this absence from home were not enough, after the fall of Troy, Ulysses was unable to return to his kingdom of Ithaca for another ten years, having been delayed by various adventures such as a near escape from the man-eating giant Cyclops and a one-year sojourn on the island of Aeaea, governed by Circe, a sorceress who turned his companions into swine. When Ulysses at last arrived in Ithaca, he found his wife Penelope importuned by a swarm of suitors, whom he drove off with the help of his son, Telemachus. The Penelope of Joyce's story, Bloom's wife Molly, has the last say in the book, a rambling monologue of several thousand words, explaining in remarkable detail how she did not reject the sexual advances of any suitor who came along, yet still kept her loyalty to her Poldy.

All the events in *Ulysses* took place on "16 June 1904" (In recent years this 16th day of June has been celebrated in Dublin and round the world – *urbi et orbi* – as Bloomsday.) The day begins with breakfast, fried bacon for Stephen Dedalus and a fried kidney for Leopold Bloom, and ends in a shared drink of Epp's cocoa in Bloom's house in Eccles Street during the early hours of the morning. Various historical events that took place on 16 June 1904 crop up in the book, such as the sinking of a ferry in New York harbour and the Gold Cup horse race at Ascot in England, but none of the events mentioned have anything to do with the nations of Ireland and Israel, which, it seems, allowed the first Bloomsday to pass without any world-stirring happening. The day marked Joyce's first meeting with his wife, but neither Sinn Fein nor the Zionist movement took any notice.

The most direct comparison of Ireland and Israel in *Ulysses* occurs in a piece of quoted oratory recited among a crowd of gossipers in a newspaper office. To a slightly sceptical eye, the oratory does not seem particularly convincing, but the piece gains an adventitious importance because it was one of four paragraphs selected by Joyce for a gramophone recording in his own voice. He must have thought it an adequate sample of his masterwork. The context is a discussion about the revival of the Irish language, one of the channels for the expression of Irish nationalism in the early years of the twentieth century, when Irish Home Rule seemed to be a lost cause, when the violence of the Fenians had burnt itself out and the violence of Sinn Fein had hardly started, and the Abbey Theatre had not yet raised the mythical banner of Kathleen ni Houlihan. It was a time for windy oratory, a time when battle lines were being drawn in nothing more permanent than the spilt beer on any pub counter.

The comparable debate in the Zionist movement at the beginning of the century concerned the use of Hebrew as the language of Jewish national revival. There was a good deal of rabbinic opposition to the use of the language of prayer as the language of political agitation. Yiddish, the language of the revolutionary socialist Bund, was recommended as more suitable. Of course, Hebrew was chosen as the language of the Zionist movement, of the kibbutzim, and of the state of Israel, and today's flourishing literature, culture, and political system demonstrate the appropriateness of the choice. The state of Eire, on the other hand, has never managed to install Irish as more than a second language, and, in spite of every encouragement, threat, and bribe, Irish is still no more than a marginal addition to the governmental system. But who was to know that Irishmen would refuse to speak Irish, who among those theorists arguing in a newspaper office in 1904 that they ought to? Or, for that matter, who could guess it in 1922 when *Ulysses* appeared? "Sufficient for the day is the newspaper thereof" (114).

The orator purports to represent a not very likely meeting between an Egyptian high priest and a youthful Moses, when the high priest, speaking like an imperialist cabinet minister, scolds the Jews for their obstinate fatuity in belonging to an inferior race.

Why will you jews not accept our culture, our religion and our language? You are a tribe of nomad herdsmen: we are a mighty people. You have no cities nor no wealth: our cities are hives of humanity and our galleys, trireme and quadrireme, laden with all manner merchandise furrow the waters of the known globe. You have but emerged from primitive conditions: we have a literature, a priesthood, an agelong history and a polity ... Israel is weak and few are her children: Egypt is an host and terrible are her arms ...
– But, ladies and gentlemen, had the youthful Moses listened to and accepted that view of life, had he bowed his head and bowed his will

and bowed his spirit before that arrogant admonition he would never have brought the chosen people out of their house of bondage, nor followed the pillar of the cloud by day. He would never have spoken with the Eternal amid lightnings on Sinai's mountaintop or ever have come down with the light of inspiration shining in his countenance and bearing in his arms the tables of the law, graven in the language of the outlaw. (117)

Elsewhere the pleasure of reading any page of this novel is made richer by reference to places and people appearing on several other pages. Here the contextless quotation from the orator is exposed as self-contradicting, self-ridiculing, and hence its absurdity can stand by itself. Are we to think of an Irish Moses coming down from Sinai with the tables of the law graven by God in Irish, only to find that not a soul among the chosen people can read them? It would make matters worse if Moses himself could not read the Hebrew commandments on the tablets and had to apply to the erudite high priest (conveniently on hand in the desert) for a translation. The first person we meet in Joyce's Dublin who is able to speak Irish is a crassly insensitive Englishman who drives Stephen out of his lodging. As for Bloom, he remembers so little of the Pesach service that his father used to read when he was a small boy that he has Moses leading the people out of Israel "out of the land of Egypt and into the house of bondage *alleluia*" (101). Israel had seen so much more of the house of bondage than of promised land that (in the year 1904 at least) it offered no good omen for Ireland. Stephen, who is one of the auditors of the citation of the windy orator, responds by suggesting that they should all go for a drink next door, and offers a story of two old women who climb Dublin's Mount Sinai — Nelson's column — and spit down secular plumstones from the top.

Stephen serves as the registrant of spoken comments about Jews, since they are rarely made directly to Bloom. The first note of anti-Semitism comes from the Britisher Haines, who is sharing a lodging with Stephen and another friend, Buck Mulligan. Haines gives voice to the common slur when he accuses "German jews" of wanting to take over his country (18). In the first decade of the twentieth century, a few Jewish capitalists were blamed for the manifold sins of British imperialist exploitation. This view is extended by Mr Deasy, the owner of a private school Stephen is temporarily teaching in. Deasy, who speaks for the Protestant [elite] in Ireland, regards his deeply rooted prejudices as equivalent to historical analysis. No doubt he would produce another collection of slanders against the Catholic Irish if the opportunity arose. "England is in the hands of the jews. In all the highest places: her finance, her press ... Old England is dying ... They sinned against the light ... And that is why they are wanderers on the earth to this day" (28). Stephen's reply is not spoken; it appears as an interior monologue and is the first example of the innovative literary method that makes this novel so remarkable. Words sounded inside the head are as much part of the ongoing situation in which they appear as would be spoken dialogue or explicit action. Stephen's memory supplies him with a view of Jewish merchants in Paris; he does not contradict Deasy's slander but picks up his false interpretation of appearances and transforms it into a lament for the impermanence of Jewish endeavours.

On the steps of the Paris Stock Exchange the goldskinned men quoting prices on their gemmed fingers. Gabble of geese. They swarmed loud, uncouth, about the temple, their heads thickplotting under maladroit silk hats. Not theirs: these clothes, this speech, these gestures. Their full slow eyes belied the words, the gestures eager and unoffending, but knew the rancours massed about them and knew their zeal was vain. Vain patience to heap and hoard. Time surely would scatter all. A hoard heaped by the roadside: plundered and passing on. Their eyes knew the years of wandering and, patient, knew the dishonours of their flesh. (28)

The reinterpretation indicates that the very stereotype that served as the hook on which prejudices were hung can be regarded, in its exotic guise, as an occasion for participation by a sympathetic observer in the sufferings of defenseless victims. Stephen goes on to produce a sentence that might be engraved as a comprehensive comment on the sorrows of the twentieth century. "History, Stephen said, is a nightmare from which I am trying to awake" (28).

Stephen's thought could well be of the long history of cruelty and suffering in Ireland. Its lapidary force speaks for all the people who look backwards only with horror and who have little hope in looking forward. But Stephen would rather not discuss Ireland. Much later in the day, drunk and battered and bored to distraction by Bloom's long-winded discourse about work for all and a tidysized income for all the Irish, Stephen in desperation interrupts, "We can't change the country. Let us change the subject" (527).

Change: "Mr Leopold Bloom ate with relish the inner organs of beasts and fowls. He liked thick giblet soup, nutty gizzards, a stuffed roast heart, liverslices fried with crustcrumbs, fried hencods' roes. Most of all he liked grilled mutton kidneys which gave to his palate a fine tang of faintly scented urine" (45).

How does a kidney manage to be attractive and repulsive at the same time? It looks interesting, it tastes nice, it slips down easily. But on second thought, it has too functional an appearance, its texture is suspiciously smooth, it lacks fibre, and the after-taste might make anyone wonder. Some people never start to like kidneys, others give them up, and those who declare themselves to be kidney-eaters do so rather defiantly. There is something about undisguised flesh-eating, something about eating a working organ, as if the sheep would like to have it back, and something, alas, to do with the production of urine, don't ask too closely. Why isn't a mutton kidney called by a different name from our own kidneys? Why doesn't it have a euphemism like "sweetbreads"? What if we decide that Leopold Bloom, here met for the first time, is somehow like a kidney? If he is, that is how James Joyce made him for his readers, his consumers. But to say a Jew is like a kidney would be an absurdity, obviously anything can be compared with anything and what sense would such a comparison make? Anyhow no Jew could be compared with the pork kidneys that Bloom enjoys for his breakfast on this memorable day.

The attempt here is to see what kind of Jew James Joyce made in Leopold Bloom.

We find out more about the mind of Bloom than of anyone else in literature, including Hamlet. Perhaps Marcel Proust says more about what goes on in his mind, but Proust is so resolutely intellectual and artistic that no thoughts that do not come up to an A level, or at least B+, are ever admitted. Whereas the thoughts of Bloom hardly ever rise above a C level, and some are frankly D or E, though never a failing F. Bloom's thoughts are never shocking or disgusting, but most of them are so ordinary, so shallow in their humdrum continuity, that the only thing that seems to be as exterior and as unremarkable as they are is the earth itself, and all the miscellaneous objects that clutter its surface. Yes, we all know that there are large forces working beneath the surface and over it – gravity here, cosmic rays out there, television in the sky, potatoes in the ground, somewhere an earthquake cooking up, and plenty of weather. But, when we look around, we see nothing of these forces, nor do we observe the beautiful landscapes that painters discover; we see trees and dogs, people and motorcars, some ordinary-looking buildings and some scraps of paper blown by the wind. Our minds are likewise stuffed with thoughts so shallow and with trivialities so boring that even a psychoanalyst would refuse to listen to them. So is Bloom's mind. But when Joyce renders the shifting spectacle of Bloom's commonplace thinking, the result is fascinating, dramatic, poignant, and above all else illuminating – a new world that reveals the whole panorama of twentieth-century living and all the potentialities of twentieth-century fiction. A reader feels like some watcher of the skies when a flying saucer skims into his ken.

Bloom's unfocused wisps of thought, which attach themselves to the sight of two horses at nosebag time, give a brief and complete sample of the impressions, judgments, and memories that pass across the surface of his mind in a second or two, more quickly than the spelt-out words. He switches from recollection to describing visual impressions because a poster advertising *Hamlet* has reminded him of Ophelia's suicide, then recalls his own father's suicide, then the day when he had to recover his father's body. But look at the horses:

He came nearer and heard a crunching of gilded oats, the gently champing teeth. Their full buck eyes regarded him as he went by, amid the sweet oaten reek of horsepiss. Their Eldorado. Poor jugginses! Damn all they know or care about anything with their long noses stuck in nosebags. Too full for words. Still they get their feed all right and their doss. Gelded too: a stump of black guttapercha wagging limp between their haunches. Might be happy all the same that way. Good poor brutes they look. Still their neigh can be very irritating. (63)

Bloom's thoughts are always transitory. A moment before thinking about his father, he had been trying to get a glimpse of a lady's legs as she climbed into a jaunting car, and had wondered why the King always dresses like a soldier for his portraits, never as a fireman or a policeman. Yet when he pauses by the pair of nags he grasps a sequence of essentials that, in Stephen Dedalus's phrase in *A Portrait of the Artist as a Young Man*, comes to "the whatness of all horse." This is because Bloom, without realizing it, is momentarily a poor brute of a horse himself. He too is a poor juggins (a simp, an easy mark), satisfied by a nosebag, bearing a rather limp stump between his legs too, with a line in repetitive talk that gets on everyone's nerves. So he catches a reflection of himself in a mirror that his thoughts have fashioned from the two horses in the street. Joyce discovered that the language of a drifting slack consciousness makes a more vividly true self-portrait the further the stream of trivialities moves beyond deliberate control.

What happens when Bloom sees himself not as a horse but as another long-nose, a Jew? Will there be a "whatness of all Jew"? As the day goes on, Bloom becomes more like Ulysses returning to Ithaca, less like a kidney-eater on the lookout for erotic adventure. His Jewishness belongs, not quite typically, to the beginning of his day. The implied recognition of Bloom and Stephen as father and son, Ulysses and Telemachus, take the form of a shared drink of cocoa and parallel arcs of urination side by side in the garden. The exchange of their Jewish-Irish identities consists of some doubtful comparisons of the Hebrew and ancient Irish alphabets, and Stephen's chanting of the folk-ballad about "the jew's daughter" who, with her little penknife, cuts off the head of a little schoolboy. Neither in fake philology nor in legends of ritual murder – age-old incitements to massacres of Jews – is there much possibility of mutual understanding. Better they not try to talk.

Both then were silent?
Silent, each contemplating the other in both mirrors of the reciprocal flesh of theirhisnothis fellowfaces. (577)

The most satisfying experience to accost Bloom during his epic day is a vision of a Zionist settlement. It originates from a picture he notices when buying his breakfast kidney. Having put the kettle on to boil, he goes to the pork butcher, Dlugacz, and, while waiting to be served, admires the vigorous hips of the servant-girl from next door who is standing in front of him at the counter. Idly picking up a piece of the cut paper that the butcher uses for wrapping, he finds a picture of cows in a "model farm at Kinnereth on the lakeshore of Tiberias" (48), and the name Moses Montefiore catches his eye. He recognizes the name but his mind wanders to mornings in the cattle market, a breeder slapping a "ripe-meated hindquarter," and by easy transition his gaze rests on the hindquarters in the skirt in front of him, inviting a lecherous mind to a slap; perhaps he will follow her into the street if the butcher hurries up. So much for Kinnereth. Instead, Dlugacz meets Bloom's eye – in spite of his pork butchering he is also Jewish – and flashes the possibility of mutual recognition, Jew meeting Jew. "A speck of eager fire from foxeyes thanked him. He withdrew his gaze after an instant. No: better not: another time" (49).

Outside in the street, the girl has gone, and Bloom's attention returns to the Zionist advertisement. The address is in Berlin – Bleibtreustrasse – Remain True Street. Can Bloom remain true to a tradition he has never known, to a community he has never entered? He can at least be true to himself, if he could find out what being a Jew means. For the moment he dreams of growing oranges in Ottoman Palestine.

Orangegroves and immense melonfields north of Jaffa. You pay eighty marks and they plant a dunam of land for you with olives, oranges, almonds or citrons ... Your name entered for life as owner in the book of the union ...
Nothing doing. Still an idea behind it.
He looked at the cattle, blurred in silver heat. Silver-powdered olive trees. Quiet long days: pruning, ripening. (49)

The vision does not last, a cloud covers the sun, and a desolate scene takes the place of the orange groves.

No, not like that. A barren land, bare waste. Volcanic lake, the dead sea: no fish, weedless, sunk deep in the earth ... A dead sea in a dead land, grey and old. Old now. It bore the oldest, the first race. A bent hag crossed from Cassidy's clutching a naggin bottle by the neck. The oldest people. Wandered far away over all the earth, captivity to captivity, multiplying, dying, being born everywhere. It lay there now. It could bear no more. Dead: an old woman's: the grey sunken cunt of the world.
Desolation.
Grey horror seared his flesh. (50)

Unlike Bloom in 1904 and Joyce in 1922, we can see that Bloom (and Joyce) chose the wrong symbol for their overwhelming sense of desolation about the future of the Jewish people, picturing the land of the first Zionist pioneers as a "dead land, grey and old." Yet, if we change the place to mid-Europe in the 1940s, the same desolation comes over us. We know too well where the "barren land, bare waste" was situated. No one could have anticipated in advance the places and the terrifying circumstances of the extermination camps. But Joyce by sympathetic imagination has made himself aware of Jewish tragedies stretching forwards as well as backwards in time; these are the grey horrors that sear Bloom's flesh. Joyce could not know about the multiplying orange groves and the dunam of land awaiting Leopold Bloom in the state of Israel.

Bloom after all is chiefly a survivor: he lives through cuckoldom and whoredom and boredom as well as anti-Semitic scorn and opprobrium. Yet on the right occasion (not frequently) he shows that he can be a fighter and stand up to persecution, wringing reluctant admiration from his detractors. As one of them says with a sneer, "Old lardyface standing up to the business end of a gun" (273).

The most notable occasion of this is called "Cyclops," from the episode in the Homeric story. Ulysses and his companions are captured by the one-eyed giant Cyclops, but they escape after Ulysses thrusts a stake into the one eye. The blinded giant hurls a rock at the retreating ship large enough to sink it, but it misses, and Ulysses survives once again. The monster in Dublin is an old and gnarled Irish patriot nicknamed "the Citizen" who sits in the corner of Barney Kiernam's pub fighting for Ireland with his ugly mouth, seconded by his repulsive dog Garryowen, and exacting his toll of pints from all comers. The episode is narrated by a despicable voice from the Dublin gutter, a collector of bad debts on behalf of a merchant called Moses Herzog. "'Circumcised?' says Joe. Ay, says I. A bit off the top" (240). Bloom is seen through the eyes of this boozer and sponger when he ventures into Kiernan's on a charitable errand, looking for a friend who will help to clear the insurance money for the widow of an acquaintance who has just died. Bloom takes no drink and does his best to agree with everyone in the idle talk that eddies round the subjects of hangmen, sport, recent trials, flogging in the navy, and the wrongs of Ireland. But he gets into trouble when he stretches the notion of "persecution" beyond indignation against the injustices perpetrated by the Sassenach, the British hyenas.

– Persecution, says [Bloom], all the history of the world is full of it. Perpetuating national hatred among nations ...
– What is your nation if I may ask? says the citizen.
– Ireland, says Bloom. I was born here. Ireland.
The citizen said nothing only cleared the spit out of his gullet and, gob, he spat a Red bank oyster out of him right in the corner ...
– And I belong to a race too, says Bloom, that is hated and persecuted. Also now. This very moment. This very instant.

Gob, he near burnt his fingers with the butt of his old cigar.
– Robbed, says he. Plundered. Insulted. Persecuted. Taking what be-
longs to us by right. At this very moment, says he, putting up his fist,
sold by auction off in Morocco like slaves or cattle.
– Are you talking about the new Jerusalem? says the citizen.
– I'm talking about injustice, says Bloom ...
– But it's no use, says he. Force, hatred, history, all that. That's not
life for men and women, insult and hatred. And everybody knows that
it's the very opposite of that that is really life.
– What? says Alf.
– Love, says Bloom. I mean the opposite of hatred. I must go now ...
– That chap? says the citizen. Beggar my neighbour is his motto. Love,
moya! He's a nice pattern of a Romeo and Juliet. (271–3)

The word "love" is not in itself conclusive or resounding, and
in its various forms, "lerv," "loov," and "luv," the sound has been
even more debased by popular songs since Joyce's day. But
"love" is a word that can mean a great deal, as the poets and
philosophers have shown us. Bloom does not make it mean very
much – he is no poet or philosopher – he is just the kind of
average man who makes everything he says or thinks irretriev-
ably ordinary, boring, banal. Yet in an unexpected way he is
making an assertion about the banality of goodness that stands
in opposition to what Hannah Arendt, in a striking phrase about
Eichmann, called "the banality of evil." What is Bloom referring
to, as far as his own experience of "love" demonstrates it? Just
a bit of kindness, consideration, thoughtfulness, a share of his
wife's bed-warmed flesh, a few lascivious thoughts, some memories of his father and of his dead son, an odd reminiscence of
"silly Milly" his daughter (as she calls herself to him); the act
of picking up someone knocked down by a bully. (It is said the
idea for *Ulysses* started when Joyce was picked up, after a scuf-
fle, by a Mr Hunter, who people said was a Jew.) How can this
banality of love stand against the whole banality of evil, against
the operating machinery of a modern state, against railways
merely being efficient, against small officials just doing their
jobs, against whole populations who, in indifference or fear, look
the other way, against the everyday habit of listening to a Mozart
quartet while terrible crimes are going on a few yards away?
Hope, Bloom seems to say, is in letting love be as humdrum,
unexciting, and uninspiring as common courtesy – and as unremarkable as casual masturbation. But never unheroic. Not
something to die for but something to survive for.

The next time Bloom pokes his head into Kiernan's pub he is attacked, though not for his words about love. Nonsensically he is accused of betting on a hot tip and making a packet from a bookmaker without standing drinks all round, as custom demands. A collection of absurd misunderstandings has added up to the situation when he is condemned for a fault and doesn't even know what he is accused of.

Mean bloody scut. Stand us a drink itself. Devil a sweet fear! There's a jew for you! All for number one. Cute as a shithouse rat. Hundred to five ...
– Don't tell anyone, says the citizen, letting a bawl out of him. It's a secret.
And the bloody dog woke up and let a growl.

(Here some of the pub loafers hold down the citizen while others get Bloom out into a jaunting car – a stand-in for Ulysses's ship. He shouts back defiantly while the citizen is "on his high horse about the jews.")

– Mendelssohn was a jew and Karl Marx and Mercadente and Spinoza. And the Saviour was a jew and his father was a jew. Your God.
– He had no father, says Martin ...
– Well, his uncle was a jew, says he. Your God was a jew. Christ was a jew like me.
Gob, the citizen made a plunge back into the shop.
– By Jesus, says he, I'll brain that bloody jewman for using the holy name. By Jesus, I'll crucify him so I will. Give us that biscuitbox here. (279–80)

This Cyclops, like his Homeric counterpart, hurled after Ulysses – Bloom – a Jacobs' biscuitbox which missed its target, so that the hero escaped. But Leopold Bloom fled from the pub in a fast car, rather in the way that Elijah ascended to heaven in a fiery chariot. "And there came a voice out of heaven, calling: *Elijah! Elijah!* And He answered with a main cry: *Abba! Adonai!* And they beheld Him even Him, ben Bloom Elijah, amid clouds of angels ascend to the glory of the brightness at an angle of fortyfive degrees over Donohoe's in Little Green Street like a shot off a shovel" (283).

Leopold deserves his apotheosis, though his escape is by no means the end of his story. But his ascent completes his specifically Jewish incarnation: he becomes less Jew and more

Greek, less Bloom and more Ulysses, a traveller like Sinbad the Sailor and Tinbad the Tailor and Jinbad the Jailer (607) and all the other alliterators.

And Leopold the Jew? The most that James Joyce seems willing to say is that Leopold survives as part of the history that makes the nightmare from which the twentieth century is trying to awake. That awakening Joyce wrote out cryptically in *Finnegans Wake*. But both Ireland and Israel did awake, however difficult and fraught with problems their awakening has been. Perhaps one day Israel and Ireland will become boring enough, banal enough, to awake into a new day of love and peace – the day when the guns will stop. Then they will persuade all the world to celebrate Bloomsday.

CHAPTER SEVEN

Literary Jews and the Breakdown of the Medieval Testamental Pattern

ROSS G. ARTHUR

In the second of the one hundred stories in his *Decameron*,[1] written in Italy during the years following the plague of 1348, Boccaccio tells the story of a learned Jew named Abraham. A friend, a rich Christian merchant, wants very much to have Abraham become a Christian, so the Jew decides to visit Rome and watch the behaviour of the pope and the cardinals to decide whether he should convert. Although his Christian friend tries to dissuade him, since he knows that the church leaders are corrupt and fears that Abraham will never change religions if he sees what is really going on, Abraham makes the trip. When he returns he has been convinced that Christianity must be the true faith and undergoes baptism. His reasons are not that he has found virtue and holiness in Rome: on the contrary, he has found greed, sexual corruption, and selfishness wherever he looked. It is this fact that wins him over, for if a religion which is so riddled with corruption and decay can survive and flourish, it obviously must be relying on and receiving direct divine aid.

In many ways, this tale highlights the problems we have in reading medieval literature to learn about medieval Jews or about medieval Christian attitudes toward Jews. It may be untypical in its humour and its biting satire, but it shares several features with other medieval stories with Jewish characters. In the first place, it contains none of the stereotyped anti-Semitic portraits that we might expect, given today's negative overtones to the word "medieval." More important, however, is the fact that the story is not really about Jews at all, not even about the Jew Abraham. Its major purpose is not to say something about Judaism, but to satirize and condemn the abuses of the papal court in a way that brackets and insulates the charges so that the author could not be condemned for anti-Christian sentiments. The stereotyped image of the Jew as a usurious, narrowly legalistic Christ-killer has its origins in the Middle Ages. But to characterize this image as "medieval" in order to distance ourselves from it, as if it could be "written out" of the present and explained away as an aberration when it appears in modern literature, is a serious distortion of medieval literary practice. The characters in many medieval texts are "types," signs of particular concepts; Jews are frequently used as signs of a particular stage in human development; and anyone, Christian, Pagan, or Jew, who exhibits certain traits can perform that particular signifying role. The role in question (Abraham's) was, in the Middle Ages, an element in a three-stage developmental plotline; this "conversion plot," as the context in which the stereotyped image was placed, did a great deal to control and mitigate the negative impact of the stock image. Once the developmental pattern was separated from the standard progression from Pagan to Jew to Christian, however, the violence inherent in the characterization lost all constraint.

Many medieval narratives are grounded in the notion that both individual human beings and the human race as a whole are on a path which leads from nature through law to grace. In the state of nature, concord between people is a matter of pure self-interest, discord is governed only by the constraints of physical strength, and speech is simply another tool for gaining one's ends, with little or no concern for factual accuracy or honourable intent. A medieval author wishing to signify this stage had many stock types at his disposal: giants, children of Cain, Pagans, "Saracens." The practice of the author of *The Song of Roland*[2] serves as a good example. The "Saracens" are shown worshiping an inverted trinity, made up of Mohammed, Termagant, and Apollyon, and this marks them as anti-Christian. When they make agreements with others, they have no intention of keeping their word and no desire to increase the general level of human harmony, but are only trying to maintain their own power through deceit; the Pagan king promises Charlemagne that he and all his people will become Christians and even offers hostages as a guarantee, but among themselves the Pagans admit that they will never do so and will sacrifice their hostages if need be. In warfare they do not play fair; they use treachery to set up a battle in which they will vastly outnumber the Christian forces in the rearguard, led by the emperor's nephew Roland.

They live in a world which is insistently physical, worshiping statues and relying on brute force; their defeat is a sign to the Christian audience that such a view is incorrect. In the process they act as Christ-killers: their chief victim, Roland, is betrayed by a Judas-figure, is willing to die in order to carry out his mission for God and Emperor, and is taken to heaven as a sign of martyrdom.

The second stage of the process is initiated by people willing to live under the rule of law. Their agreements are not temporary matters of policy but permanent covenants — two parties state what they will do and affirm that they will adhere to their promises. Discord is governed by the rule of strictly equivalent retribution: "an eye for an eye" was seen, by Augustine and others, as a principle restraining the "natural" human impulse to respond to an injury with a far greater injury. Speech is judged according to factual accuracy: the truthful person is the one whose words correspond with the facts as they are and whose promises are carried out to the letter. A medieval author wanting to depict this stage quickly and recognizably would create a character who is a Jew; more often than not, of course, such an author would show greater interest in the problems and contradictions thought to be inherent in such a view of human action in the world. The spirit behind equal retribution is often shown to be as vicious as that of the original crime, and adherence to "the letter" of a promise is often far from satisfying to someone who had a different understanding of the words when they were first spoken.

The third and final stage which these authors imagined was analogous to the theologian's idea of grace and mercy. Within a narrative world tolerably close to the real world of the audience, the perfected Christian hero speaks words whose intent is to increase harmony in the world and love of one's fellow man, gives all that he has to ensure concord, and refuses to repay evil for evil. Struggles with renegades are intended to bring about their reformation, not to exact vengeance, and free gifts are made for the benefit of others, where in the second stage there were only mercantile bargains to ensure mutual gain. Such a stage is most easily depicted in the person of a saint or a hermit, but the static nature of such characters relegated them to minor roles in most secular narratives, so that in most romances this level is best observed in characters who have reached it, arduously, after experiencing difficulties in living in the first two worlds.

The Pagan, the Jew, and the Saint are the stereotyped images
of these three stages. They correspond to three stages in the
history of the whole human race as seen by medieval thinkers,
and to three stages in the spiritual development of the individual. In fact, rather than being present in stories of Pagans who
first convert to Judaism and then to Christianity, this pattern is
most often exemplified in the stories of individuals who are nominally Christian but start off their careers, in the narrative, at
one of the "earlier" stages and move toward the goal that has
been set for them through a carefully ordered sequences of partial successes and setbacks. Conversely, other literary characters, even some whom later criticism calls "heroes," never
complete the developmental process and even backslide into
the world of self-interested agreement and physical "overkill"
in response to injury. An examination of a few such narratives
will display more clearly the background into which Jews, and
the characteristics medieval authors ascribed to them, were
placed.

The "eye for an eye" pattern, in which violent action is the
dominant topic, is examined, for example, in *Sir Gawain and the
Green Knight*.[3] The court of King Arthur is presented as a group
of knights with a state-of-nature desire for combat between two
knights, as a kind of entertainment: the Christmas festivities
cannot really begin until some adventure has come to the court
or there has been a fight between two knights willing to risk
their lives. The "adventure" that arrives, however, is an enig-
matic Green Knight, who introduces the rule of law into the
narrative in the form of a challenge to balance violent actions
in precisely equivalent terms: one of Arthur's knights is to strike
him, and then, a year later, to receive an equivalent blow in
return. Although Gawain decapitates him, the Green Knight
does not die, and Gawain is contractually obliged to submit to
justice, according to the principle of "a head for a head." While
he is on his way, as he thinks, to his death, he makes another
covenant with a man who gives him lodging: at the end of each
day, each man will give the other what he has won. Gawain
fulfils this promise for two days, but on the third, he keeps a
supposedly magical girdle his host's wife has given him, believing that it will save his life. Despite his breach of the "law,"
Gawain is spared by the Green Knight: under the terms of their
agreement, he could cut off Gawain's head, but instead he
merely nicks his neck, as "penance" for keeping the girdle. The
audience has seen a series of tableaux depicting lawless nature

superseded by the rule of law which is fulfilled in the free gift of grace.[4]

The covenant pattern is presented in a twelfth-century romance by Chrétien de Troyes called *Yvain*.[5] The hero, who has married the widow of a knight whom he killed in combat, under rather dubious circumstances, promises his wife that he will return to her after a one-year period of chivalric jousting and adventure. He forgets the time, thereby breaking his covenant, and so loses her love. His remorse causes him to regress to a period of solitary, animal-like wandering; this is followed by a regeneration signified by a succession of more and more altruistic adventures. Finally he is granted her love again, by her free choice, rather than by right of conquest as before. First he wins the woman by violence, then he comes to deserve her through just actions, then he receives her love as a free gift.

The "letter of the law" pattern is manifested in the tale told by the Franklin in Chaucer's *Canterbury Tales*.[6] While her husband is away, a woman agrees, in jest, to commit adultery with a young man if he can remove all the rocks from the coastline, rocks which symbolize for her the dangers threatening her travelling husband. Much later, with the help of a magician, the young man succeeds and calls upon the lady to be true to her word. Her husband even insists, over her protests, that her honour depends on fidelity to the letter of her promise, so she goes to the young man, ready to do his bidding. He is so moved by her self-sacrifice that he frees her from her bargain, and in return he is released from his debt to the magician. Once it begins to operate, the spirit of mercy spreads, and we are left with the hope that the woman's marriage, presented initially as a bargain based on equivalent exchanges, will henceforth be grounded in a more spiritual gift of love.

For a modern reader, none of these stories has any connection with Jews or Judaism at all. Yet for a medieval reader, the themes of covenant, equivalent justice, and literalism carry overtones of the Christian view of the Old Testament. This is the background, the literary background at least, against which medieval stories about Jews need to be examined.

Despite the common-sense modern view, medieval writers saw no contradiction between the Old Testament commandments and their re-interpretations in the New Testament. The first covenant was not abrogated, but fulfilled in the second; the letter of the law was not abolished, but transmuted into the spirit; and the injunction to turn the other cheek was seen as a fulfilling progression from the principle of restraining oneself to an equivalent retribution, not as a contradictory commandment. The Old Testament was regarded as the word of God, and hence true, although in need of spiritual exegesis in order to be properly understood; to argue either that it could be understood in a purely literal way or that it had been completely replaced by the New Testament was regarded as dangerous heresy.

The place imposed upon the Jews by this scheme was ambiguous. They were not, like Moslems, assimilated to pure evil, since the book in which they believed was seen as divinely inspired and not, like the Koran, regarded as a fabrication by a renegade and heretical human. Literary Jews were therefore condemned by Christians not for belief in something false but for stubborn adherence to the letter of their text in the face of pressure to accept the Christian version of its spiritual meaning. This view of Jewish beliefs goes back at least to the Gospel of John, where Jews are shown insisting on a clumsily literal interpretation of Jesus' metaphorical statements, and where "Jew" has become almost a technical term for those who refuse to accept him as the messiah. Jesus himself is presented, quite unhistorically, as referring to the Jews as "they," as if he was not one of them.

Nevertheless, at least in the earliest of the medieval English texts, a certain respect is shown for the knowledge, wisdom, and scholarship of the Jew. When, in Cynewulf's *Elene* (ninth century), the mother of the emperor Constantine comes to Judea in order to find the true cross, she summons "a thousand men of discerning mind in a throng such as were most completely familiar with ancient tradition among the Jews." The important Jews, in this narrative, are therefore those who are most aware of and obedient to Jewish law; the "Christ-killers" are the Jews of the past, who actually plotted the crucifixion, not their descendants. Once the scholars have assembled, Elene addresses them, attempting to win them over through arguments based on standard Christian proof texts from the Old Testament:

Listen, you of discerning mind, to the divine mystery, the word and the wisdom. Now, you have received the teaching of the prophets, how the Author of life was born in the form of a child, the mighty Ruler, of whom Moses, defender of the Israelites, sang and said these words: "To you shall be born in obscurity a boy renowned for his powers, whose mother shall not grow pregnant with offspring through a man's love-making." Of him King David, the wise prophet, Solomon's father, sang a noble song, and the warrior's lord declared these words: "I have kept before my gaze the God of creation and Lord of victories. He, Ruler of the hosts, has been in my sight, and the glorious shepherd has been at my right hand; from him shall I not turn my face ever to eternity."[7]

Finally, one of their number, appropriately named Judas, is singled out for special attention, and after a great deal of resistance that the empress meets with stern force, he reveals the location of the three crosses. When he arrives at the spot where they are buried, he asks for a sign to show whether or not Jesus was truly God's son. When the pleasant smoke he requests rises from the ground, Judas is convinced. In order to determine which of the three crosses is the right one, and which are those of the two thieves who were crucified with Jesus, they raise them, one by one over a corpse, at the precise hour when Jesus died: "Then the third one was lifted up in its holiness. The corpse was in waiting until the Prince's cross was reared above him, the tree of the heaven-King, the true emblem of victory. At once he rose up, furnished with his spirit, body and soul both together. There was seemly praise exalted among the people; they honoured the Father, and extolled aloud the true Son of the Ruler: 'To him be glory and the thanks of all creatures for ever without end.'"[8] In due course, Judas is baptized, takes the name Cyriacus (here etymologized as "the Saviour's revelation") and becomes a bishop who ministers to the converted Jews and spreads the word. In this poem, the negative image of the Jew is present only in the Christ-killers of the historical past, while the "good Jews," loosely corresponding to the positive images which Deborah Heller has found in Dickens and Eliot, are here those who are open to the possibilities of ceasing to be Jews at all: even Satan can see that while he once had a sort of victory through the actions of another Judas, this Judas has now furthered the process of his defeat.

   The function of such a work is to strengthen the faith of its Christian audience, not to make a statement to or about Jews in the poet's society. At every stage in the poem, concern is shown for the process by which Christian belief spreads, first to the emperor Constantine through a vision of the cross, then to his mother, then to Judas and his compatriots, and then to the poet and his audience. This process may be accomplished through divinely granted visions, through human persuasion, through a combination of persuasion, force and miracles, or through inspired reading of religious texts. The goal of the process is summed up in Cynewulf's prayer: "May the gate of hell be closed and heaven's unlocked and the realm of angels opened everlastingly, may their joy be eternal and their portion assigned them with Mary, for everyone who holds in remembrance the festival of the most precious rood beneath the skies which the most mighty, the sovereign Lord of all, overspread with his arms."[9]

This pattern, which was seen as optimistic by its original users, did not survive completely intact, although the broad outline of the paradigm endured. By the mid-fifteenth century, several of the elements in the structure were being presented in a much more negative form, although the ultimate goal of the narrated events was still described in glowingly positive terms. The Croxton *Play of the Sacrament*, most likely written shortly after 1461 when the events it describes were reputed to have happened, sees Jews not just as resistant to Christian beliefs concealed behind Jewish texts but as malevolently opposed to Christian doctrine. A Jewish merchant named Jonathas, who is described as a follower of the laws of Mohammed, refuses to accept the Christian belief in transubstantiation: "The belief of these Christian men is false, as I think; for they believe in a cake – I think it is unnatural. They say that the priest binds it, and by the power of his words makes it flesh and blood – thus by a conceit they would make us blind – and that it is the one who died upon the cross."[10] To test and disprove this foolish belief, he arranges to buy a piece of consecrated bread from Aristorius, a Christian merchant. The merchant keeps insisting that he would not sell it for a hundred pounds, but when Jonathas's offer rises from twenty pounds, to forty pounds, and finally to one hundred pounds, Aristorius agrees. This extended bargaining could be seen, from the medieval point of view, simply as a sign that Jews operate by contract and as an indication of spiritual blindness, for Jonathas says openly that he wants to buy "your almighty God, in a cake." But the insistence on the monetary and mercantile nature of the contract is also an indication of the Renaissance stereotype of the Jew as a usurious merchant who is not properly grateful for this material possessions in the world: unlike the Christian, who thanks and worships God for his prosperity, Jonathas thanks Mohammed before he goes into a thirty-two line description of all of his valuable property.

Once they have obtained the mass-wafer, through the help of Aristorius and the negligence of a priest, the Jews place it on a table, and after a mocking rehearsal of Christian belief, they attack it with daggers. In this period, then, the Jews who are of interest to the narrative *are* Christ-killers, for they re-enact an attack on Christ's body in the host. When it bleeds, they decide to throw it into a boiling cauldron, but it clings to Jonathas's hand. His servants nail the bread to a pillar and try to pull him away from it, but his hand breaks off. The violence and the resistance continue until a crucifix appears above the fiery furnace, and Jesus commands them to stop their blasphemy. All the Jews instantly convert and confess to a bishop, in whose presence the speaking crucifix is transformed back into the wafer. Jonathas's hand is healed, he and the other Jews are baptized, and Aristorius and the careless priest are assigned proper penance.

Once again, despite the undoubtedly negative and vicious portrayal of Jonathas and his servants, the major concern of the play is not with either Jews or Judaism. Early critics found it difficult to connect this play to social conditions in England in the period, where there had been no Jews for almost two hundred years. The explanation is, as before, that the stage Jews are simply playing a part in a story whith a Christian didactic purpose. The virulent anti-Semitism of the French, Dutch, and Italian analogues has been muted and subordinated to an argument in favour of those parts of Catholic doctrine which were under assault from the English Lollards. These early Protestants denied transubstantiation, condemned the veneration of crucifixes and other images, and denied the necessity of oral confession to a priest. All of these points of doctrine are "proved" by the action of the play, and the Christian author has delivered his message to his Christian audience. [11]

Despite the striking differences in tone and the substitution of the merchant role for the scholar role, the structure of *The Play of the Sacrament* still exhibits strong similarities to that of *Elene*, even after the passage of over five hundred years. In both works, in order to strengthen or reform the belief of their audiences, the authors tell stories about Jews whose quarrel is not with individual Christians but with Christian beliefs. The goal of the Christian characters and the end point of the narrative is the conversion of the Jews, not their punishment or destruction, and this is effected by means of a miracle. The doubt and resistance of the Jews is overcome in the story so that doubt and heresy may be removed from the Christian audience.

The persistence of at least the basic elements of this optimistic plot line makes it all the more difficult to understand Chaucer's *The Prioress's Tale*, written some seventy years before *The Play of the Sacrament*, or to see it as an indication of Chaucer's own point of view rather than as his display of the errors of the Prioress. In the Prioress's narrative, Jews are presented not only as opponents of Christian doctrine but also as vicious murderers of an innocent little boy who walks through the ghetto singing a Latin hymn in praise of the virgin Mary. The Prioress goes to great lengths to make her audience sympathize with this boy and with his poor mother, pulling out all the emotional and rhetorical stops available. Despite the fact that the boy's throat has been cut, he continues to sing his hymn, and the Christians are therefore able to find his body and give it proper burial, after brutally killing all the Jews who knew anything at all about the boy's death.

This plot is a grotesque parody of the pattern in *Elene* and *The Play of the Sacrament*. Instead of leading to the spread of faith and Christian charity, the miracle which Mary provides does nothing more than allow the Christians to exact mindless vengeance. There is no possibility for conversion, and even the Christian audience is invited to become obsessed with evil, not to become aware of mercy. Even though it is expressed in terms of equal and opposite justice, the Christian provost's statement, "For evil must have evil's just desert,"[12] leads rather to a "state of nature" overkill in which many people are punished, by being first torn apart by horses and then hanged. The progression is not from vengeance to law to mercy, but quite the reverse.

Despite the difficulties in seeing this work as representing Chaucer's attitude toward Jews, it is also not possible to believe that his primary purpose was to expose and criticize the evils of anti-Semitism. Rather, the violence and repulsiveness of the conclusion of the Prioress's story focus attention on her deficient understanding of Christian doctrine. The inversion of the traditional pattern shows that she does not comprehend the functioning of salvation history. The root cause of her difficulties is her over-valuation of simple faith, the "innocence" whose dangers Allen Koretsky has demonstrated, and her corresponding lack of interest in the need for active works of charity. Her hero is not a person with a firm belief grounded in knowledge of doctrine, but a completely passive child who merely sings words

in praise of Mary without even understanding the language in
which they were written. Throughout both her prologue and her
tale, the Prioress shows an excessive regard for miraculous powers and no concern at all for what can be done by human efforts.
Similarly, the Jews in her story do not perform their actions of
their own free will, but are presented simply as pawns for Satan,
who inspires them to put a stop to the boy's perceived insult.
They are much more like the Moslems in the *Chanson de Roland*
or in Chaucer's *Man of Law's Tale* than like the Jews of the
salvation history narratives, and foreshadow in a frightening
way the Satanic portraits of Shylock and Fagin. In fact, the
Prioress is not even as optimistic as the authors and tellers of
the stories about Pagans, since in them many of the previously
evil Moslems are converted, whereas her tale ends only with
destruction. The Prioress sees life as a battle between the forces
of good and the forces of evil, but it is carried on exclusively by
supernatural opponents, with the humans being little more than
puppets. If we can see Chaucer as depicting the errors of the
Prioress through this tale, then the optimistic pattern was still
in force and had value for him, even though his manner of revealing this was through a demonstration of the ugliness which
ensues when the paradigm is inverted by a storyteller whose
faith is merely passive.

By the late sixteenth century, however, the tensions that result from using an identifiable social group to play a part in a
mythic structure had reached the breaking point. This can be
seen in two Renaissance dramas which can justly be said to
present anti-Semitic portraits of Jews, Shakespeare's *The Merchant of Venice*[13] and Marlowe's *The Jew of Malta*.[14] Although a
modern reader's dominant memories of *The Merchant* will be of
Shylock and the pound of flesh, it is possible, at least for a
medievalist, to imagine a version of its plot in which his role is
radically reduced or even played by someone other than a Jew.
The entire fifth act, aftr all, unfolds without any reference to
him or to the "bond plot" in which he is a central figure. Such
a story would be analogous in structure to Chrétien's *Yvain*. In
the casket plot, Bassanio wins Portia in marriage through his
successful completion of a task he accepts in a covenant made,
in effect, with Portia's dead father: she is granted to him in
return for his choice of the correct casket. She involves him in
another covenant, with herself this time rather than her father,
when she gives him her ring and exacts his promise never to
give it away. When he does give it away, to the disguised Portia

in gratitude for her rescue of Antonio, it is not a sign that he loves Antonio more than he loves Portia, but an indication from the author to the audience that gratitude and love, as concerns of the spirit, are more important than the adherence to the letter of any contract. Further, as a result of Bassanio's breach of contract, Portia is made completely free to follow the dictates of her heart; at the end of the play it is clear to everyone that she is married to him because she wants to be, not because she must.

In a medieval or even early Renaissance work, Shylock and the bond plot would have been clearly subordinated to this pattern. The mercantile bargain with Antonio, which establishes the equivalence between a pound of flesh and the money he lends, and his insistence on taking exactly what was promised rather than any amount of money, could be seen as underlining the stagnancy of contractual relationships and the self-destructiveness of adherence to the letter of an agreement. But Shylock's story contains too many gratuitous negative details to allow us to see it only in such a subsidiary manner. Shylock is not led away from his concern with contracts and the letter into a belief in mercy, and none of the Christian characters shows him any of the mercy about which Portia speaks so eloquently. Rather, to the principle of "those who live by the sword shall die by the sword" is applied to him. The "letter" of his contract allows him to take only one pound of flesh, but no blood; the impossibility of following such a plan exactly is used to stop him, according to his own literalist principles. What is more, a law of Venice which punishes any alien who threatens the life of a citizen is brought against him, and all that he values is taken from him. He is not converted spiritually, by persuasion, divine vision, or miracle, but rather by force, as part of a punishment rather than as an entry into what either the author or the audience could see as a positive new stage of development. The implication is clear that, by this point in history, the mythic pattern of salvation history is appropriate only to Christians, not to Jews at all. They are no longer seen as representatives of an Old Testament way of thinking which may be fulfilled in the acceptance of New Testament ideals, but could be shown as a collection of materialistic and mercenary people who deserve whatever punishment is meted out to them. Shylock's basic humanity, as discussed by Derek Cohen, has its effect on a modern audience, but leaves the characters in the play unmoved.

Despite the fact that the name of Shylock has come to be synonymous with the Renaissance stereotype of the vicious Jew, he cannot hold a candle to the greedy and destructive Barabas in Christopher Marlowe's *The Jew of Malta.* His wickedness is apparent from his murderous and treacherous deeds in the course of the play, but what is perhaps more effective is his self-definition, early in the action, when he allies himself with a Moor named Ithamore:

> As for myself, I walk abroad a-nights,
> And kill sick people groaning under walls;
> Sometimes I go about and poison wells;
> And now and then, to cherish Christian thieves,
> I am content to lose some of my crowns,
> That I may, walking in my gallery,
> See 'em go pinioned along by my door.
> Being young, I studied physic, and began
> To practise first upon the Italian;
> There I enrich'd the priests with burials,
> And always kept the sexton's arm in ure
> With digging graves and ringing dead men's knells ...
> Then after that was I an usurer,
> And with extorting, cozening, forfeiting,
> And tricks belonging unto brokery,
> I fill'd the gaols with bankrupts in a year,
> And with young orphans planted hospitals.[15]

He is presented as a perfect counterpart to the evil Moor, who has spent his life

> In setting Christian villages on fire,
> Chaining of eunuchs, binding galley slaves.
> One time I was an hostler in an inn,
> And in the night time secretly would I steal
> To travellers' chambers, and there cut their throats.
> Once at Jerusalem, where the pilgrims kneel'd,
> I strewed powder on the marble stones,
> And therewithal their knees would rankle so
> That I have laugh'd a-good to see the cripples
> Go limping home to Christendom on stilts.[16]

Barabas's response to the similarity between their natures and past careers is to make Ithamore his companion, since they are both circumcised and both hate Christians. In this work, the salvation history pattern is completely lost, and the literary Jew is associated not with a stage of development, but with the ir- redeemable evil, and the "Jew as Satan" motif as firmly estab- lished, all but obliterating the image of the Jew as guardian of the Law. To make the process complete, Marlowe evokes the name of Machiavelli, so that Barabas is connected not only with mythic evil but with the man who represented all that was con- sidered evil in contemporary political practice. Each of these negative characteristics, as has been shown above, took on a life of its own over the succeeding centuries.

The examination of these texts, from the perspective of lit- erary history, reveals the period from 900 to 1600 as a time of steady disintegration of a formulaic "happy ending" plot line and the progressively negative depiction of one of its elements. This conclusion, however, becomes quite disturbing when we move beyond that narrow scholarly point of view. First, the increas- ingly vicious portrayal of Jews coincides with another devel- opment in narrative technique, one which modern readers generally consider a positive step, both in literature and real life. In the medieval texts all the characters, Jewish or Chris- tian, are presented not as individual humans with lives and personalities of their own, but as flat "types," playing out their roles according to predetermined patterns. It is only with the increased interest in depicting "well-rounded" people that char- acters such as Shylock and Barabas become possible; they begin a developmental process that leads to Fagin and the usurious manipulators in Trollope's works. We must ask whether the gains outweigh the losses when authors shift their focus from plot to the individualized characters so valued by modern read- ers.

The second problem with a positive evaluation of the medieval pattern emerges when we step outside the bounds of purely literary study. For whom is the ending "happy"? Only for literary characters, who have no real existence. Who defined "happy"? The Christian author and the Christian audience. What is the real source of the power to label the Hebrew Scriptures as the "Old" Testament and to declare what their "spiritual" meaning is? What would be the effect of such stories on an audience, as opposed to the intention we may deduce from a purely literary analysis? We may surmise that a medieval Christian who took these stories seriously would treat real Jews the way stage Christians treat stage Jews. What would happen when there was no real miracle to correspond to the stage miracle, when no one was raised from the dead and no crucifix spoke, and the real Jew did not convert? A Renaissance Jew could perhaps improve his position with Christians by convincing them that he was not like Shylock or Barabas, but a medieval Jew who obstinately refused to follow the literary pattern of Judas and Jonathas would be signing his own death warrant. How can we be sure that Chaucer's audience would be able, without the benefit of footnotes and the leisure to examine other texts and to evaluate his intentions, to see that he was not inciting hatred against Jews? It was, after all, during the medieval period that accusations of ritual murder against the Jews brought about their expulsion from England, and performances of the continental analogues to *The Play of the Sacrament* resulted in anti-Jewish riots. On the other hand, it was shortly after the productions of *The Merchant of Venice* and *The Jew of Malta* that Jews were allowed to return to England. Just as the placement of a stereotyped image in the full literary context of a narrative complicates the understanding of that image and confounds any attempt at simplistic analysis, then, the recognition that literary activity takes place in a complex social environment forces continual re-evaluation of the uses both poets and critics make of stock characters and stock plots in their communication with their audiences.

Notes

1 On the first page of her important study of the Prioress, published over twenty years ago, Florence Ridley carefully warns
readers about interpretations of Chaucer that are based more on
the perceptions, values, social structures, and political ideologies of the twentieth century than on those of the fourteenth:
"Unconsciously, most of us expect to find in our favorite authors
attitudes sympathetic to our own; and today we seem to look for
tolerance of minority groups above everything else. Such an attitude is, of course, a commendable part of our national conscience but it does not appear to have been one that Chaucer
shared with us or embodied in his 'Prioress's Tale.' In view of the
religious intolerance of the poet's own time and place this should
surprise no one; it would have been most unlikely for a fourteenth century English poet to satirize a nun and a legend of the
Virgin in order to attack anti-Semitism" (*The Prioress and the
Critics* [Berkeley: University of California Press, 1965], 1). It is
interesting to note that this same scholar, in an article published
five years after her monograph on the Prioress, recognizes Chaucer's abiding moral relevance as one of the poet's most appealing
characteristics for us today: "For five hundred and seventy-eight
years readers have felt an instant response to Chaucer's characters, a sudden electric sense of recognition, in part because the
poet depicts basic human experience, reactions, and types"
("Chaucerian Criticism," *Neuphilologische Mitteilungen* 81[1980]:
133).

   While I readily accept Professor Ridley's point about the danger of reading Chaucer unhistorically, that is, unmindful of the

context of fourteenth-century English culture, and, while I do not for a moment claim that Chaucer was a champion of oppressed minorities (a kind of medieval civil libertarian), I do believe that Chaucer intended the Prioress to be, at best, a morally ambiguous character.

2 George Lyman Kittredge, for instance, ignores it completely in his discussion of *The Prioress's Tale*, in *Chaucer and his Poetry* (Cambridge, Mass.: Harvard, 1915), 175–80. G.K. Chesterton, despite more than a dozen references to the Prioress in his book *Chaucer* (London: Faber and Faber, 1932), passim, also ignores the unpleasant subject of anti-Semitism: cf. the typically early twentieth-century response to the Prioress of G.G. Coulton, who notes "the fine black cloth and snowy linen of Madame Eglantine and her fellow nun, clean and dainty and demure ... Her [the Prioress's] dignified reserve, her natural anxiety to set off a fine person with more elaboration of costume than the strict Rule permitted, her French of Stratford atte Bowe, her tenderness to lapdogs and even to marauding mice, her faultless refinement of behavior under the ticklish conditions of a fourteenth-century dinner-table – all these pardonable luxuries of a fastidious nature are described with Chaucer's most delicate irony" (*Chaucer and His England*, 5th ed. [London: Methuen, 1930], 147).

3 All quotations from Chaucer in this paper are from *The Riverside Chaucer*, ed. Larry D. Benson et al., 3rd ed. (Boston: Houghton Mifflin, 1987).

4 See, for instance, James Parkes, *The Conflict of the Church and the Synagogue* (1934; repr. NY: Atheneum, 1979) and *The Jews in the Medieval Community*, 2nd ed. (NY: Hermon, 1976); R.J. Schoeck, "Chaucer's Prioress: Mercy and Tender Heart," in *The Bridge, A Yearbook of Judaeo-Christian Studies*, vol. 2, ed. John M. Oesterreicher (NY: Pantheon, 1956), repr. in *Chaucer Criticism, The Canterbury Tales*, ed. Richard J. Schoeck and Jerome Taylor (Notre Dame, Ind.: Notre Dame, 1961), 245–58; Cecil Roth, *A History of the Jews*, rev. ed. (NY: Schocken, 1974); and Leon Poliakov, *The History of Anti-Semitism*, trans. Richard Howard (NY: Schocken, 1974).

5 Albert B. Friedman, "The *Prioress's Tale* and Chaucer's Anti-Semitism," *ChauR* 9 (1974): 119.

6 See page 13.

7 Muriel Bowden, *A Reader's Guide to Geoffrey Chaucer* (NY: Farrar, Straus, 1964), 50–1.

8 Germaine Dempster, *Dramatic Irony in Chaucer* (1932; repr. NY: Humanities Press, 1959), 336.

9 Friedman, "*The Prioress's Tale* and Chaucer's Anti-Semitism,"
   121.
10 See Kittredge, *Chaucer and his Poetry*, 175–7; Sister Mary
   Madeleva, *Chaucer's Nuns and Other Essays* (NY: Appleton,
   1925), 3–29; and John M. Manly, *Some New Light on Chaucer*
   (NY: Holt, 1926), 202–20.
11 Robertson, *A Preface to Chaucer* (Princeton: Princeton University
   Press, 1962), 248.
12 Robert Worth Frank, Jr, "Miracles of the Virgin, Medieval Anti-
   Semitism, and the Prioress's Tale," in *The Wisdom of Poetry*,
   ed. Larry Benson and Siegfried Wenzel (Kalamazoo, Mich.: Medieval Institute Publications 1982): 178.
13 Beverly Boyd, ed., *The Middle English Miracles of the Virgin*
   (San Marino, Calif.: Huntington Library, 1964), 113.
14 Gregory Baum, "Introduction," in *Faith and Fratricide*, Rosemary
   Ruether (NY: Seabury Press, 1974), 3.
15 Baum, "Introduction," 12.
16 Ruether, *Faith and Fratricide*, chap. 3, esp. 170–81.
17 John Chrysostom, *Eight Orations Against the Jews*, as quoted in
   ibid., 179.
18 "Laws of Constantius, August 13, 339," in *The Jew in the Medieval World*, ed. Jacob R. Marcus (1938; repr. NY: Atheneum,
   1981), 5.
19 "Medieval Spanish Law and the Jews, Las siete partidas," in *The
   Jew in the Medieval World*, 38.
20 Roth, *A History of the Jews*, 198.
21 Barbara W. Tuchman, *A Distant Mirror: The Calamitous Fourteenth Century* (NY: Ballantine, 1978), 112–13.
22 Frank, "Miracles of the Virgin," 292 n.8.
23 Florence Ridley, "Chaucerian Criticism," *Neuphilologische Mitteilungen* 8 (1980): 133.
24 The weight and complexity behind the phrase *Amor vincit omnia*
   are evident in even the simplest glosses of modern editors.
   A.C. Baugh translates the Latin as follows: "Love (divine) con-
   quers all" (*Chaucer's Major Poetry* [NY: Appleton-Century-Crofts,
   1963], 241 n.1. John Fisher notes that the phrase is proverbial,
   but he reminds us as well, by his reference to the occurrence of
   the phrase in Virgil's *Tenth Eclogue*, that the word *amor* had a
   purely secular, erotic meaning in Antiquity (*The Complete Poetry
   and Prose of Geoffrey Chaucer* [NY: Holt, Rinehart, and Winston,
   1977], 12 n. to l. 162). E.T. Donaldson believes that the phrase,
   in the context of the portrait of the Prioress, is probably deliberately ambiguous, encompassing both earthly love and the love of

God ("Commentary," in *Chaucer's Poetry*, ed. E.T. Donaldson [NY: Ronald, 1958]: 884–5.

25 This reference has led to a psychoanalytic study by Maurice Cohen, "Chaucer's Prioress and her Tale: A Study of Anal Character and Anti-Semitism," *Psychoanalytic Quarterly* 31 (1962) 232–45.

26 Alfred David, *The Strumpet Muse* (Bloomington: Indiana University Press, 1976), 209.

27 Ibid., 208–9.

28 Robertson, *A Preface to Chaucer*, 242, 247.

29 John Gardner, *The Poetry of Chaucer* (Carbondale, Ill.: Southern Illinois University Press, 1977), 306.

CHAPTER TWO

1 Introduction, *The Merchant of Venice*, The Arden Edition (London: Methuen, 1964), xxxix.

2 Leo Kirschbaum, *Character and Characterization in Shakespeare* (Detroit: Wayne State University Press, 1962), 19.

3 Bernard Grebanier, interestingly enough, agrees that the play is not anti-Semitic, but contains instances of anti-Semitism. He remarks that Gratiano "is the only character in the entire play who can be accused of anti-Semitism." *The Truth about Shylock* (NY: Random House, 1962), 300.

4 All references to *Merchant* are taken from *The Riverside Shakespeare*, gen. ed. G. Blakemore Evans (Boston: Houghton Mifflin, 1974).

5 Lucy S. Dawidowicz, *The War Against the Jews 1933–1945* (NY: Holt, Rinehart and Winston, 1975), 29.

6 Ibid., 222.

7 John Palmer, *Political and Comic Characters of Shakespeare* (London: Macmillan, 1962), 401–39; Harold C. Goddard, *The Meaning of Shakespeare* (Chicago: University of Chicago Press, 1960), 81–116.

8 Quoted by Lawrence Danson, *The Harmonies of The Merchant of Venice* (New Haven and London: Yale University Press, 1978), 130.

9 Albert Wertheim, "The Treatment of Shylock and Thematic Integrity in *The Merchant of Venice*," *Shakespeare Studies* 6 (1970: 75).

10 John P. Sisk, "Bondage and Release in *The Merchant of Venice*," *Shakespeare Quarterly* 20 (1969): 217.

11 Toby Lelyveld, *Shylock on the Stage* (Cleveland: Press of Western Reserve University, 1960), 8.

12 A fuller analysis of these two critical readings is provided in Danson, *The Harmonies of the Merchant of Venice*, 126–39.

13 Kirschbaum, *Character and Characterization in Shakespeare*, 26.

14 Gordon Craig, "Irving's Masterpiece – 'The Bells,'" *Laurel British Drama: The Nineteenth Century*, ed. Robert Corrigan (NY: Dell, 1967); 119.

CHAPTER THREE

1 Edgar Johnson, *Charles Dickens: His Tragedy and Triumph* (Boston and Toronto: Little, Brown and Co., 1952), vol. 2, 1010.

2 Cited in Harry Stone, "From Fagin to Riah: Jews in the Victorian Novel," *Midstream* 6 (1960): 29, 30. The citations of the Davis-Dickens correspondence that follow are also taken from Stone's excellent article. For the originals, see Dickens, *Letters*, Nonesuch Dickens (London, 1937–38), 12, 357 and Cecil Roth, *Anglo-Jewish Letters* (London, 1938), 304–9. References to the correspondence also appear in Edgar Johnson, "Dickens, Fagin, and Mr. Riah," *Commentary* 9 (1950): 49–50; Montagu Frank Modder, *The Jew in the Literature of England* (New York and Philadelphia, Meridian Books Inc., and The Jewish Publication Society of America, 1960), 220; Edgar Rosenberg, *From Shylock to Svengali: Jewish Stereotypes in English Fiction* (Stanford, Calif.: Stanford University Press, 1960), 16, 37, 134–5; Frank A. Gibson, "The Impossible Riah," *Dickensian* 62, 349 (1966): 188; and Mark Gelber, "Teaching 'Literary Anti-Semitism'; Dickens' *Oliver Twist* and Freytag's *Soll und Haben*," *Comparative Literature Studies* 16, no. 1 (1979): 4.

3 Modder accepts Dickens's retrospective profession of good faith uncritically, see 220, 223. Johnson recognizes some of the complexities of the problem but concludes, "Artistically, of course, Dickens' explanation on the subject of Fagin had been completely sound. *Oliver Twist* had expressed no sentiments against the Jews as a people, and there was nothing in the delineation of Fagin any more representative of them than Squeers was of men with only one eye or Uriah Heep of men with red hair" ("Dickens, Fagin, and Mr. Riah," 50).

4 These "Jewish" and "non-Jewish" traits in Fagin have been well observed by other critics; discussions of Fagin's "Jewishness" can be found in Stone, "From Fagin to Riah," Rosenberg *From Shylock to Svengali*, and Lauriat Lane, Jr, "Dickens' Archetypal Jew," *Publications of the Modern Language Association of America* (PMLA) 73 (1958): 94–100, and in the same author's "The Devil in

Oliver Twist," *Dickensian* 52 (1956): 132–6. Johnson, "Dickens, Fagin, and Mr. Riah," stresses the non-Jewish elements in Fagin, as does Steven Marcus, though he also acknowledges some "Jewish" elements in the character: "Who is Fagin?" *Dickens from Pickwick to Dombey* (NY: Simon and Schuster, 1965): 358–79. Gelber has more recently handled the same considerations with a different emphasis ("Teaching 'Literary Anti-Semitism,'" 1–11).

5 The fullest and most important account of Fagin as a Jew-devil can be found in Lane, "Dickens' Archetypal Jew." Also see Lane, "The Devil in Oliver Twist," Rosenberg, *From Shylock to Svengali*, and Harry Stone, "*Oliver Twist* and Fairy Tales," *Dickens Studies Newsletter* 10, nos. 2 & 3 (1979): 34.

6 Charles Dickens, *Oliver Twist*, ed. Peter Fairclough, with introduction by Angus Wilson (Great Britain: Penguin Books Ltd., 1966), 105. Future page references to the novel will be to this edition and will be included in the text.

7 A depressing compendium of these charges can be found in Joshua Trachtenberg, *The Devil and the Jews* (Philadelphia: The Jewish Publication Society of America, 1983). Also see Lane, "Dickens' Archetypal Jew" and "The Devil in *Oliver Twist*," and Rosenberg, *From Shylock to Svengali*.

8 Marcus makes a great deal of these "hypnagogic" states in his psychoanalytic reading of Fagin's role in the novel ("Who is Fagin,") ff. 370.

9 In his insistence on winning Oliver over to his party through the boy's voluntary choice, Fagin had, incidentally, resembled a French red-headed devil-in-human form, a literary contemporary who is, similarly, after a young hero's soul. Two years before Dickens's *Oliver Twist*, Balzac in *Le Père Goriot* had created the satanic Vautrin (an alias for the master criminal, Jacques Collin), who seeks the freely chosen allegiance of the young Eugène de Rastignac – though the French devil's conformity to his mythic role is motivated by an element of sexual self-interest not present in Fagin. (A contrary view of Fagin as pederast – for which I fail to see any convincing evidence – is presented by Gary Wills, "Love in the Lower Depths," *New York Review of Books*, 26 October 1989, 60–7, and by Angus Wilson's more muted suggestion in his introduction to the Penguin edition of the novel, 22.) Vautrin's satanic lineage, moreover, is not medieval but Romantic. Hence he sees himself as a pupil of Rousseau, speaking out against "the bottomless hoax of the Social Contract," and he is seen by his associates as the "their Bonaparte." When betrayed into the hands of the police (by treachery likened to that of Ju-

das), Vautrin is described by Balzac as "a poem of Hell," and "the fallen archangel"; his capture is the occasion for his rhetorical and moral triumph, as he eloquently proclaims his superiority to the "flabby limbs of a gangrenous society." This is a very different moral from that implied in Fagin's arrest, which represents the vindication of an essentially just and moral social order. For Dickens's villains have none of the heroic glamour of the social rebel, nor is Fagin encumbered by any of Vautrin's intellectual baggage. Of course, we should remember that, though a red-headed devil, (who, unlike Fagin, tries to conceal his red hair under a black wig), Vautrin is not Jewish. Honoré de Balzac, *Le Père Goriot* (Paris: Garnier-Flammarion, 1966), 187, 176, 186. Translations are my own.

10 Lane, "Dickens' Archetypal Jew," 100 and Lane, "'Oliver Twist': A Revision," *The Times Literary Supplement*, 20 July 1951, 450.

11 Edmund Wilson, *The Wound and the Bow* (NY: Oxford University Press, 1965), 53.

12 See Stone, *"From Fagin to Riah,"* 25, 21–2, to whose article I am also indebted for my account in the subsequent two paragraphs of recorded changes in Dickens's attitude toward Jews. For a fuller history of the Jews in England in this period, see Cecil Roth, *A History of the Jews in England* (Oxford: Oxford University Press, 1978), 240–66.

13 In addition to Stone, *"From Fagin to Riah,"* 24, see Johnson, "Dickens, Fagin, and Mr. Riah," 48.

14 In addition to Stone, *"From Fagin to Riah,"* 29, these items from Dickens's correspondence are cited in Lane, "Dickens' Archetypal Jew," 98.

15 Charles Dickens, *Our Mutual Friend*, ed. Stephen Gill (Great Britain: Penguin Books Ltd., 1971), 328. All future citations of the novel will be to this edition and will be included in the text.

16 Again, for a different view of Fagin, see Gary Wills, "Love in the Lower Depths," and Angus Wilson, "Introduction."

17 It is, however, possible to overestimate the role of the Jewish moneylender in the Middle Ages. "The heyday of the Jewish predominance in the world of finance was from the middle of the twelfth century ... A century later, the Gentile usurer (legal and canonical restrictions notwithstanding) once more became a universal, though highly unpopular figure. Legal fictions were found to get round the impracticable regulations ... Against the activities of these Christian competitors, with their august patronage and their vast cooperative resources, the Jew was utterly powerless, and before long he was driven to the wall." Cecil Roth, *A History of the Jews* (NY: Schocken Books, 1961), 194–5.

18 Rosenberg, *From Shylock to Svengali*, 69.
19 It should be apparent here that my argument is fundamentally at
odds with Rosenberg's contention that "the Veneerings, the
Lammles, and their sort, who have adopted all the sordid upstart
traits associated with 'Jewish capitalism' ... are probably themselves thinly veiled portraits of Jews" (269). In a note Rosenberg
states his case more strongly, while attributing the point to
Lane: "the Veneerings, Lammles, and their sort ... are unmistakably odious Jews" (342). Actually, Lane is much more cautious,
only pointing to some anonymous financial friends of Mr Lammle,
mentioned once, "(mostly asthmatic and thick-lipped) who were
forever demonstrating to the rest, with gold pencil-cases which
they could hardly hold because of the big rings on their fore-
fingers, how money was to be made (bk. 2, chap. 9)." Lane concludes: "Here, put forth casually and parenthetically, is the very
oversimplification Dickens was trying to attack through the character of Riah!" "Dickens Archetypal Jew," (99). More sweep-
ingly, Rosenberg, having asserted (though attributing the idea to
Lane) that the Veneerings and the Lammles "are unmistakably
odious Jews," then faults Dickens's novel for the fact that these
"portraits of Jews ... personify the very vices that elsewhere in
the same novel the cloddish Riah is explicitly made to repudiate"
(269). Lane's cautious reminder that Dickens may have shared
some of the anti-Semitic prejudices he was trying to correct may
be well taken; Rosenberg's suggestion that Dickens didn't know
what he was about in the structure of his novel seems to me in
error. Dickens was not stupid. Moreover, his distrust of vulgarity
and financial unscrupulousness was part of a profound critique of
– nominally Christian – Victorian social and economic life, a critique in which anti-Jewish feeling was simply not involved.

CHAPTER FOUR

1 Anthony Trollope, *The Prime Minister*, 2 vols. (NY: Oxford University Press, 1951), 1: 163.
2 Anthony Trollope, *The Way We Live Now*, 2 vols. (NY: Oxford
University Press, 1983), 1: 31. All quotations are from this edition.

CHAPTER FIVE

1 George Eliot, *Daniel Deronda*, ed. Barbara Hardy (Great Britain:
Penguin Books Ltd., 1967), 436. All future citations of the novel

will be to this edition, and hereafter page references will be given in the text.

2 Montagu Frank Modder, *The Jew in the Literature of England* (Philadelphia: The Jewish Publication Society of America, 1939), 288. For a fuller study of the Jewish response to *Daniel Deronda* – the ways in which it was reviewed, discussed, translated (often selectively) – see Shmuel Werses, "The Jewish Reception of Daniel Deronda," *Daniel Deronda: A Centenary Symposium*, ed. Alice Shalvi (Jerusalem: Jerusalem Academic Press, 1976), 11–47.

3 Edgar Rosenberg, *From Shylock to Svengali: Jewish Stereotypes in English Fiction* (Stanford, Calif.: Stanford University Press, 1960), 184; Alice Shalvi, *Daniel Deronda*, 8.

4 For example, from Dr Hermann Adler, Rabbi of Bayswater Synagogue, London, and from David Kaufmann, a professor at the newly established Jewish Theological Seminary in Budapest, and subsequently author of an appreciative study, *George Eliot and Judaism* (1888).

5 All citations of the letters are taken from the Yale Edition [7 vols.], *The George Eliot Letters*, ed. Gordon Haight (New Haven: Yale University Press, 1954–55).

6 Henry James, "*Daniel Deronda*: A Conversation," *Atlantic Monthly* 38 (December 1876): 684–94; reprinted in *George Eliot: A Collection of Critical Essays*, ed. George R. Creeger (Englewood Cliffs, NJ: Prentice Hall Inc., 1970), 172.

7 F.R. Leavis, "Introduction," George Eliot, *Daniel Deronda* (NY: Harper Torchbook, 1961), xviii. See xiv-xviii for his "correction" of James.

8 F.R. Leavis, *The Great Tradition* (NY: New York University Press, 1963), 12.

9 Hardy, Introduction to *Daniel Deronda* 19.

10 Rosenberg, *From Shylock to Svengali*, 163.

11 H.R.S. Van der Veen, *Jewish Characters*, cited in ibid., 48.

12 Hardy, "Introduction," 15.

13 William Baker, "George Eliot and Zionism" in Shalvi, *Daniel Deronda: A Centenary Symposium*, 53.

14 "German Wit: Heinrich Heine," *Westminster Review* 65 (January 1856). Matthew Arnold's essay on Heine, more widely known today, appeared in 1863. Eliot's essay "probably did more than any other single work in introducing to English-speaking peoples the genius that was Heine's." S.L. Wormley, *Heine in England* (Chapel Hill, 1943), 113; cited in Gordon Haight, *George Eliot: A Biography* (NY and Oxford: Oxford University Press, 1968), 193.

15 Born in Silesia, Deutsch had come to London from Germany in
    1855 to work as a cataloguer of books for the British Museum.
    He wrote a widely acclaimed article on the Talmud for the
    Quarterly Review in 1867, of which he sent George Eliot a proof.
    For a brief account of Deutsch, and George Eliot's relation to
    him, see Haight, *George Eliot*, 407, 469–71.
16 For a detailed study of George Eliot's long-standing interest in
    Judaism, see William Baker, *George Eliot and Judaism* (Salzburg,
    Austria: Institut für Englische Sprache und Literatur, 1975).
17 In terms of the individual, this view informs all of George Eliot's
    fiction. In terms of political and social life, this view is implicit
    throughout *Daniel Deronda*, and is also expressed explicitly in
    Mordecai's speeches as well as in George Eliot's subsequent es-
    say, "The Modern Hep! Hep! Hep!," written against anti-Semi-
    tism and in favour of Zionism, which appeared a couple of years
    after her last novel: "The eminence, the nobleness of a people,
    depends on its capability of being stirred by memories, and of
    striving for what we call spiritual ends – ends which consist not
    in immediate material possession, but in the satisfaction of a
    great feeling that animates the collective body as with one soul
    ... not only the nobleness of a nation depends on the presence of
    this national consciousness, but also the nobleness of each indi-
    vidual citizen." George Eliot, "The Modern Hep! Hep! Hep!,"
    Impressions of Theophrastus Such (Toronto: George N. Morang
    and Co. Ltd., 1902), 148, 149.
18 Rosenberg has discussed the Lapidoth-Mirah relation as an at-
    tenuated link to the "Jew's daughter" theme, familiar to us from
    The Merchant of Venice, The Jew of Malta, and *Ivanhoe* (168–70),
    to which we may also add *The Way We Live Now*, discussed in
    the previous chapter. Intriguingly, as with Mirah and Lapidoth,
    Deronda's relation to his mother, to which we shall presently
    turn, can be seen in part as an inversion of this stereotype; here,
    the virtuous child espouses rather than flees from Judaism, while
    the reprehensible parent has sought, by contrast, to escape a
    Jewish identity.
19 The exception is the Meyrick family, whose son Hans, "daringly
    christened after Holbein" (221), is a painter and studies abroad,
    while his mother and sisters reveal a true appreciation of culture
    at home. But Mrs Meyrick is half French.
20 George Eliot's choice of the name Klesmer has been praised by
    her Jewish critics as indicative of her thorough knowledge of
    things Jewish, since it means itinerant musician in Yiddish,
    though it had meant the musical instrument itself in Hebrew.

21 Rosenberg, *From Shylock to Svengali*, 173.
22 *Letters* II, 86, 396. See also *Letters* V, 58: "I feel too deeply the difficult complications that beset every measure likely to affect the position of women and also I feel too imperfect a sympathy with many women who have put themselves forward in connexion with such measures, to give any practical adhesion to them. There is no subject on which I am more inclined to hold my peace and learn, than on the 'Women Question.' It seems to over-hang abysses, of which even prostitution is not the worst ... But on one point I have a strong conviction ... And that is, that women ought to have the same fund of truth placed within their reach as men have" (4 October 1869). For a recent, sympathetic discussion of George Eliot's relation to the women's movement of her day, see Gillian Beer, *George Eliot* (Bloomington: Indiana University Press, 1986), chap. 6.
23 Haight, *George Eliot*, 396.
24 And while she is the only woman in George Eliot's fiction to ex-press the conflict between creative self-fulfillment and mother-hood, we might legitimately be tempted to speculate whether George Eliot's own decision not to have children may have had sources beyond her irregular – in Victorian terms – relationship with Lewes.
25 *Letters* IV, 298.

CHAPTER SIX

1 All references to *Ulysses* are to the Penguin edition of the cor-rected text, ed. Hans Walter Gabler with Wolfhard Steppe and Claus Melchior (Harmondsworth, Middlesex, England: Penguin Books Ltd, 1986).
2 Richard Ellmann, *Ulysses on the Liffey* (NY: Oxford University Press 1972), 186.

CHAPTER SEVEN

1 Giovanni Boccaccio, *Il Decamerone*, ed. G. Petronio (Torino: Ei-naudi, 1966); *The Decameron*, tran. John Payne, rev. C.S. Single-ton (Berkeley: University of California, 1982).
2 *La Chanson de Roland*, ed. J. Bédier (Paris: L'Edition d'Art H. Piazza, 1937); *The Song of Roland*, tran. R. Harrison (NY: Mentor, 1970).
3 *Sir Gawain and the Green Knight*, ed. J.R.R. Tolkien and E.V. Gordon, rev. N. Davis (Oxford: Clarendon, 1967); *Sir Gawain*

and the Green Knight, tran. B. Stone (Harmondsworth: Penguin, 1974).

4 Ross G. Arthur, "A Head for a Head: A Testamental Template for *Sir Gawain and the Green Knight* and *The Wife of Bath's Tale*," *Florilegium* 6 (1984): 178–94.

5 Chrétien de Troyes, *Le Chevalier au Lion (Yvain)*, ed. Mario Roques (Paris: Champion, 1978); translated in Chrétien de Troyes, *Arthurian Romances*, tran. D.D.R. Owen (London: Dent, 1987).

6 Geoffrey Chaucer, *The Riverside Chaucer*, ed. Larry D. Benson (Boston: Houghton Mifflin, 1987); translated in Geoffrey Chaucer, *The Canterbury Tales*, tran. D. Wright (Oxford: Oxford University Press, 1985).

7 Cynewulf, *Elene*, ed. P.O.E. Gradon (London: Methuen, 1958), 11. 333–49; translated in *Anglo-Saxon Poetry*, ed. S.A.J. Bradley (London: Dent, 1982).

8 *Elene*, 11., 883–93.

9 *Elene*, 11., 1228–35.

10 *The Play of the Sacrament (Croxton)* 11., 199–204 (modernized); in *Medieval Drama*, ed. D. Bevington (Boston: Houghton Mifflin, 1975).

11 Cecilia Cutts, "The Croxton Play: An Anti-Lollard Piece," *Modern Language Quarterly* 5 (1944): 45–60.

12 Wright's translation of line 632 (1822).

13 W. Shakespeare, *The Merchant of Venice*, ed. J.R. Brown (London: Methuen, 1961).

14 C. Marlowe, *The Jew of Malta*, in *Complete Plays and Poems*, ed. E.D. Pendry (London: Dent, 1976).

15 Marlowe, II, iii, 176–90.

16 Marlowe, II, iii, 205–14.

Index

Contributors

Ross G. Arthur teaches comparative literature in the Humanities Department at York University, Toronto. He is the author of *Medieval Sign Theory and Sir Gawain and the Green Knight* (Toronto: University of Toronto Press, 1987) and articles on medieval narrative poetry. He is currently involved in research on French and Provençal adventure romances.

Derek Cohen teaches English at York University. He is the author of *Shakespearean Motives* (Macmillan, 1988) and articles on seventeenth-century drama and contemporary South African literature.

Harry Girling has taught at the University of Witwatersrand, South Africa, and is Professor Emeritus of English at York University in Toronto. He has published articles on Henry James, Commonwealth Literature, linguistics, and editorial methods.

Deborah Heller teaches comparative literature in the Humanities Department at York University. She has published articles on nineteenth- and twentieth-century English and European writers, including Wordsworth, George Eliot, Mme de Staël, Ibsen, Dickens, and Kafka, and has recently contributed essays to two books on women in Italian literature.

Allen C. Koretsky teaches English at York University. His special interests are medieval literature and eighteenth-century fiction. He has published on Chaucer and Richardson. He is also at present Master of Stong College in York University.